Great Expectations

Great Expectations

How to Make 30 Easy, Fast, Sexy, Cheerful
Maternity Outfits That Let You Feel Like
a Woman as Well as a Mother-to-Be

Leigh Adams and Lynda Madaras

Illustrations by Marianne Anderson

Photos by Margaret Grundstein

Houghton Mifflin Company   Boston   1980

Hopelessly dedicated to David and Beau

— L.A.

*And to my daughter, Area, who's in all my dedications and to
Frank whose psychic abilities saved the day and to Steven for
flaming banana crêpes at midnight and to Debra Cappiobiance
who taught me how to spell.*

— L.M.

Copyright © 1980 by L. Leigh Adams and Lynda Madaras

Library of Congress Cataloging in Publication Data

Adams, Leigh.
    Great expectations.

    1. Maternity clothes.   2. Sewing.   I. Madaras,
Lynda, joint author.   II. Title.
TT547.A23   646.4′04   80-14036
ISBN 0-395-29460-6

Printed in the United States of America

AL 10 9 8 7 6 5 4 3 2 1

Book design by Edith Allard, Designworks, Inc.

Contents

Introduction

Basics

Quickies

Recycled

Introduction

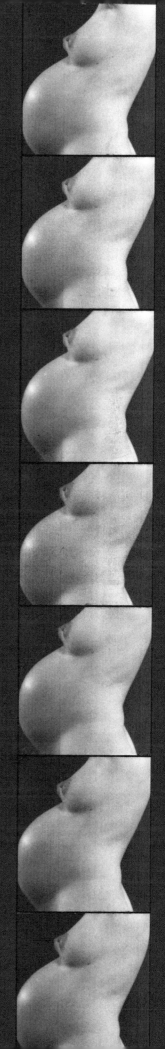

If You've Got It, Flaunt It

It used to be that pregnant women kept a low profile — at least as far as that was possible, given their condition. In many cultures, ranging from polite, white-glove societies to primitive tribal organizations, pregnant women are actually exiled from public view. Indeed, at one time, if you were pregnant, you stayed put, within the confines of your own home and did not appear in public.

Nowadays, we've supposedly "come a long way, baby," but when you start to look at the kinds of clothing available for pregnant women, you begin to wonder just how far we've really come. Most maternity clothes are designed to hide or camouflage the fact that the wearer is pregnant. Huge, tentlike constructions with yards of material and enough gathers to conceal the belly of a pregnant elephant are the norm. Hiding bellies is not the only curious thing about maternity clothes. Traditionally, maternity clothes tend to be rather little-girlish in design. They are fraught with frills, ribbons, ruffles, and bows. Tiny prints full of teeny animals and other such nonsense that would delight the heart of a five-year-old are typical. Polka dots and pastel pinks abound.

Why do we attempt to hide pregnancy and clothe the obviously sexually experienced woman as if she were a little girl? The answer to this question probably lies in murky Oedipal depths and in our cultural embarrassment about sexuality. But, enough of this. It's time for a change, and that's what this book is all about: fresh new designs for a whole new kind of maternity clothes.

No belly-hiding little-girl fashions here. The clothes in this book are from the "If you've got it, flaunt it" school of design. In place of the usual parachutelike garments we've created soft, sensual clothes that mold to the contours of a pregnant body. We've replaced the shapeless garments that stretch from belly to rear end in awkward lines with free-flowing constructions that hang gracefully. Instead of the outdated, frumpy, childish designs, we created smart, chic, fashionable clothing.

We hope that the clothes in this book will help you feel attractive during your pregnancy and enjoy the new way your body looks. It isn't always easy to feel attractive when you're pregnant. The overriding cultural image of pregnancy is one of a fat, waddling, duck-like creature. Don't buy that; instead, use the designs in this book to create a new image of sensuality, grace, and elegance.

Most of us have enough vanity to enjoy the way we look dressed up in clothing we like. It's especially important to support your vanity when you're pregnant. Our self-images depend at least in part on the messages we get from those around us.

A friend of ours tells a very funny story about how she was strolling down the street one day, in her ninth month, wearing a dress de-signed by Omar-the-tentmaker. A gang of construction workers on their lunch break were "girl-watching," tossing comments of ap-proval in typical pubescent, adolescent fashion at passing females. As she walked past there was dead silence, until she was about to round the corner, when one of them let loose with a long, low, wolf whistle. "It really broke me up. I turned back and yelled, 'Thanks, I needed that!' We all laughed, and it was true, I really did need it."

Unfortunately, pregnant women are apt to get some very strange messages from the people around them. We've encountered peo-ple, usually men, who find the sight of a pregnant woman repulsive and disgusting (Oedipal depths, no doubt). Luckily, there are plenty of people who don't feel this way, but, remember, this is a culture that's still into hiding pregnancy. The waddling, fat duck image is a pervasive one. You'll need a lot of ammunition to defend yourself from old images and strange messages. So, don't fall into the trap of wearing your mate's old clothes and schlepping around in an ugly polyester parachute because you hate to spend the money on something you'll only wear when you're pregnant. Try making some of the clothes in this book, most of which can be worn after pregnancy as well. In fact, make a whole closetful. It will be the best investment you've ever made.

If you find yourself slipping into the oh-I'm-so-fat-and-ugly blues, spend some time pampering yourself. Massage oils on your belly or, better yet, get someone to help you. Doing this every day, espe-cially on the lower belly and thighs, will keep your skin supple and elastic and will feel good. Or, light a candle and sit or lie comfort-ably, just looking at your body. Watch the play of the candlelight on your rounded contours, the soft glow it casts over the horizon of your Buddha belly. If you're the adventurous type, you might do something a friend of ours recommends: paint floral designs on your belly with body paints. It's at least guaranteed to give your gynecologist a giggle.

We highly recommend nude photo sessions. Not only are the photos something you'll treasure in years to come, but they'll also help your self-image. On the back of the snapshot put the date and, occasionally, weight and measurements. It'll be something to chuckle about when you can see your toes again.

Pregnant bodies really are beautiful and a camera can help you see that beauty with fresh eyes. The photos here are of a friend who was feeling a little low, but once she saw the prints, she began to feel a whole lot better about herself.

By all means, get a full-length mirror and spend some time admiring your changing body each day. You'll need one anyway to admire the exciting new wardrobe you'll be creating with the help of this book.

Criteria

The clothes in this book were selected on the basis of several criteria. First of all, they had to be designs that were not little-girlish or belly-hiding, and they had to be attractive, chic even. We wanted clothes that would hang well on pregnant bodies. We especially wanted to avoid the balloon effect of so many maternity clothes. We didn't want garments that pulled across the belly and rear end, thereby making a pregnant body look awkward. Then, too, they had to be comfortable.

Next, we wanted them to be versatile. We looked for basic garments that could be dressed up or down and that could be personalized to suit any woman's lifestyle, whether it was urban career woman, suburban housewife, or rural earth mama. We also wanted clothes that could be worn after the baby comes as well.

And last, but not least, we wanted these clothes to be simple to make, so simple that a complete novice could pick up the book and actually be able to successfully complete a wearable garment.

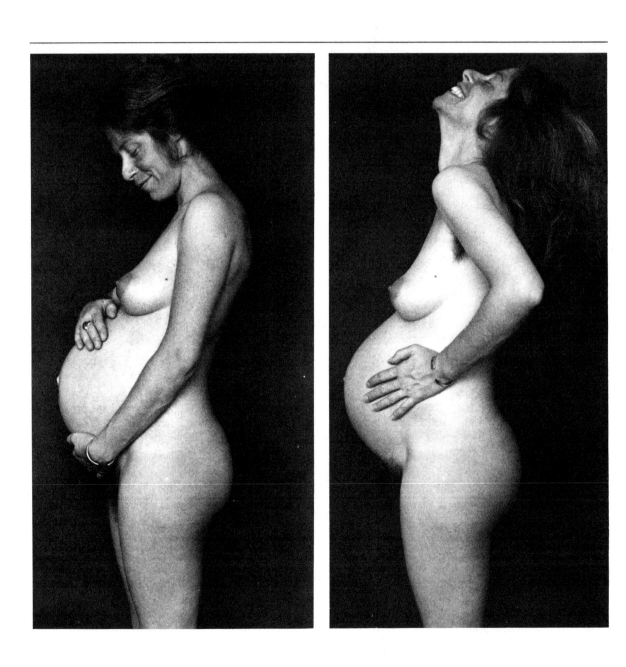

The patterns in this book are organized in three different sections: Basics, Quickies, and Recycled. The Basic section includes a kaftan, a wraparound dress, a yoke dress, a skirt, a pair of pants, a vest, and a cape. The kaftan and dresses can be transformed into coats, blouses, jackets, and robes with just a few simple alterations in the basic pattern. The pants, vest, and skirt can be made in different lengths to suit your needs. The cape is also a versatile garment — it can be worn in a number of different ways. The patterns in this section can be modified to create an entire wardrobe. The second section includes a number of dresses, pants, skirts, and so on, all of which are quite easy to make. In fact, some of them require only a few stitches and a few minutes to make. The final section will show you how to use scarves, sheets, pillowcases, tablecloths, towels, and blankets to create an entire wardrobe of recycled finery.

Sewing Tips

If you're new to the world of sewing, we think you'll find the instructions in this book quite easy to follow. We've tried to eliminate all the fancy details and much of the confusing sewing lingo to make the whole affair less intimidating.

The best source for information on sewing matters is that walking encyclopedia of sewing knowledge, the salesclerk in your local fabric shop. So, if you're attempting your first garment, bring this book along, show the clerk what you want to make and ask for pointers, suggestions, advice, and wisdom. But, just so you'll know enough to ask the right questions, read through the following pages to learn about some of the basics.

Selecting your fabric

Basically, there are two kinds of fabrics, knit ones and woven ones. The fabric you select is, of course, a matter of personal choice, but keep things like laundering and cleaning requirements in mind when choosing your fabrics. Our favorite fabric by far is Qiana, which is a soft, comfortable, easy-care knit fabric that hangs beautifully on a pregnant body. If you are buying a knit fabric, though, you will need to use a special needle and thread. If you are a novice, don't hesitate to ask the salesclerk's opinion and advice regarding your fabric choice.

Preparing the fabric

Probably the biggest mistake beginners make is ignoring the all-important step of preparing the fabric. Even though you're excited about your project and eager to start sewing, hang on to your enthusiasm and pay some attention to preshrinking your fabric and straightening the edge and grain or you'll end up with an ill-fitting garment, full of strange lumps, wrinkles, and folds.

With all the new fabrics and fabric finishes on the market, you'd think that shrinkage would be a thing of the past, but not so. Luckily for you, you're pregnant and the clothes you'll be making are not close-fitting ones, so with most fabrics you won't have to worry too much about shrinkage. Cotton, linen, and other woven fabrics, however, will have to be preshrunk. The most reliable method of determining whether or not the fabric you've chosen is a woven one that will require preshrinking is by holding it up and asking the salesperson. In addition, the salesperson can give you specific laundering instructions for preshrinking your particular fabric. If necessary, iron your fabric before you begin to work with it.

The next step is to fold your fabric in half so that the *selvage edges,* the narrow, uncut, woven bands on either edge of the fabric, are even. Then, keeping the edges even, smooth your fabric out so that it lies flat, which you probably won't be able to do. This is because the grain of your fabric is off. *Grain* refers to the direction of the threads or yarn that makes up your material. Basically, fabrics are composed of hundreds of threads running down and hundreds going across. Your fabric is *on grain* when the crosswise and lengthwise threads are at perfect right angles to each other. If your fabric is off grain, you can straighten it by pulling the fabric in the opposite direction from the way it is slanted. (Fig. 1.)

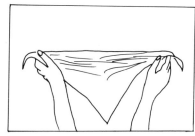

Figure 1

By examining fabric, reading labels, and kibitzing with the salesclerk, you'll discover that some permanent finish fabrics, certain knits for instance, can never be straightened. It's perfectly OK to use them as they are. You may find some printed fabrics that are off grain — avoid them!

Next, you'll need to straighten the raw edges (the cut edges) of your fabric. If you're working with a woven fabric, you can notch a selvage edge, pull a crosswise thread so that it puckers slightly, and cut along that line. With knitted fabrics, you can sometimes straighten the edge by cutting along the pattern line of the fabric, or you can use a ruler. To check to see that your woven fabric is even, pull a thread off one of the raw edges. The thread will come right off if the fabric is straight and the edges even. (Fig. 2.)

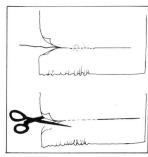

Figure 2

Making your pattern

To make many of the garments in this book, you must first make a pattern. To make the patterns, you'll need pattern paper with a 1-inch grid, which costs about thirty cents a yard and can be purchased at a good fabric shop. If you have trouble finding pattern paper, you can order it from Mary Wiggins, ℅ Home Silk Shop, 330 North La Cienega Boulevard, Los Angeles, California 90048.

The sized patterns in this book are small, medium, and large. Your pregnant size is the same as the size you were before you were pregnant. This may sound a bit ridiculous, but what we mean is that if you were a small size prior to pregnancy, select the small size pattern. You may want to check your size by cutting the pattern pieces from an old sheet, pinning the pieces together, and checking fit before you cut into ten-dollar-a-yard fabric; however, most of these garments have enough leeway in their design so that fitting isn't too critical a problem.

To make your own pattern, simply transpose from the small grid patterns in this book to the larger grids of your pattern paper. If you duplicate, square by square, you'll be able to reproduce the pattern quite accurately. If, for instance, a line bisects a square at a certain angle on the small pattern grid, you should draw a line that bisects the larger square of your pattern at just the same angle. Any markings, grainlines, or centerpoints on the patterns in this book should likewise be transferred to your pattern.

Pinning

The following hints will help you with pinning:

. Make sure your fabric lies flat and even on a smooth surface.
. Pin the fabric every 6 inches or so along the fold and along all edges and selvages; and, if necessary, clip the selvage every few inches so that the fabric will lie perfectly flat.
. Use a ruler to make sure that the grainline directional arrow on your pattern is parallel to the selvage edges.
. Pin pattern pieces to the wrong side of the material when working with folded fabric, the right side when working with a single layer.

. Pin first along lengthwise grain and fold lines.

. Place your pins perpendicular to and ¼ inch inside the edge of the pattern and diagonally at the corners.

. Space your pins every 3 or 4 inches or closer for sheer or slippery fabrics.

. Avoid lifting the fabric from the table while pinning.

Layouts and special fabrics

The pattern layouts in this book will show you how the various pattern pieces should be pinned to the fabric; however, certain types of fabric will require special layouts.

Napped fabrics like fleece are brushed after weaving to produce a fuzzy directional surface on one side. The fabric will feel rough when you move your hand against the nap and smooth when you move with the nap. *Pile* fabrics like velvet are actually made so that some of the yarns rise at an angle from the woven surface. Both types of fabric produce a different color and texture according to the direction of the nap or pile. Cut with the nap running down for a lighter, shinier look; with the nap running up for a darker, richer color. When working with pile or nap fabric, you will want to pin your pattern to the wrong side of the fabric so that the pattern paper won't shift while you're working.

There are also certain fabrics that have a woven or printed design with a definite one-way, up-down direction. Certain textured fabrics like satin and brocade have to be treated just like pile, nap, and one-way designs because of the way light is reflected off their surface causing a shading effect. All of these fabrics must be laid out on a single layer of fabric and cut so that pattern pieces are placed in the same direction. This usually means that you will need extra yardage since having to run everything in the same direction can handicap your attempts to use your yardage most economically. Here again, that fountain of knowledge, the salesclerk in the fabric store, can help you figure out the required layout pattern and how much extra yardage will be required.

Fabrics with a border print require a little extra thought as well and may require extra yardage. If, for instance, you want your border to fall at the hemline of a dress or skirt, choose a fabric with a border running along one lengthwise edge and place it where the hem will fall. When the pattern is laid out along the crosswise grain, the garment can only be as long as the width of the fabric (fabric comes in three standard widths: 36 inches, 45 inches, and 60 inches). Figure out where you want your finished hemline to fall and pin the pattern to the fabric so that the border and hem are aligned. Match the design at the side seams when possible. If the border has a dominant motif, place it at the center in the front and back.

If you are working with a large-scale print, you will also want to pay special attention to how you lay out your pattern pieces. Here again, you may need extra yardage. For a pleasing visual effect, it is best to center large-scale designs vertically. Usually the dominant motif is placed in the center front and back of the bodice and in the center of the sleeve. Unless you have a fairly bizarre sense of fashion, you'll probably want to avoid placing large circles, flowers, and the like, on your derrière or bust. Some large-scale prints have a definite vertical or horizontal pattern and, thus, may fall into the one-way category mentioned above.

Plaids and stripes are about the most troublesome patterns to work with, and we recommend that beginners, especially pregnant ones, avoid them; however, if you've got your heart set on plaids or stripes, the all-knowing salesclerk will be able to help you figure extra yardage and the proper cutting layout. We, however, refuse to aid and abet a pregnant woman attempting to make a striped or plaid garment.

Cutting

The following tips will help you with cutting out your pattern pieces:

. Never cut until you've first pinned all the pattern pieces in place.
. Cut on a flat surface.
. Avoid moving the material as much as possible.
. Use long, even strokes and cut accurately.
. Fold the cut pieces softly and lay them gently on a flat surface.
. Cut all pattern pieces, linings and facings as well, at the same time.

Marking

Although there are other methods available, we use tailor's chalk or fabric-marking pencils to mark pattern pieces. Most of the marks on the patterns in this book are near the edges, so it is a simple matter to unpin the pattern, fold it back, and mark the fabric. You can also use a dressmaker's wheel and special carbon paper to mark your patterns. Any of these marking implements can be purchased at a good fabric store.

The most critical marking in most of the patterns in this book is centerpoints. You can find the centerpoint of a piece of fabric by folding it in half or by using a measuring stick. We prefer the folding, just because it's easier; however, if you are working with a heavyweight fabric or one that doesn't have a smooth surface, the ruler or yardstick method sometimes works better.

Stitches   There are any number of hand and machine stitches that can be used in making clothing, but we've tried to limit ourselves to a few basic ones.

Running Stitch
This stitch is the most basic of all the hand stitches. It can be used for easing, gathering, mending, sewing seams, applying trims, bindings, and for tacking things in place. Insert the needle and thread through the fabric to be stitched and bring it out again a fraction of an inch farther along (fig. 3); take several small forward stitches, being careful to weave the needle in and out of the fabric evenly before you pull the thread all the way through. Pick up as many stitches as your fabric and needle will allow. For permanent seams, stitches should be ¹⁄₁₆- to ¹⁄₈-inch long; for basting and gathering, ¹⁄₁₆- to ¹⁄₄-inch long. (Fig. 4.)

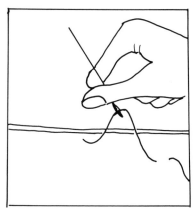

Figure 3

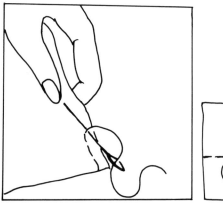

Figure 4

Slipstitch

This stitch is used to join two pieces of fabric together, especially when you want little or no stitching to show. Working from right to left, start with the thread pulled through the upper fold. About ¼ inch from there, take up a thread or two of the fabric immediately below the fold. (Fig. 5.) Move along another ¼ inch and insert the needle right through the fold and bring it out again without letting it pierce the outer side of the fabric. (Fig. 6) Pull the thread through. (Fig. 7.) Then, moving along another ¼ inch, pick up a thread or two from the fabric immediately below the fold. (Fig. 8.)

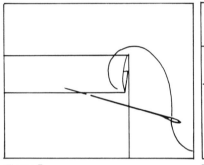

Figure 5

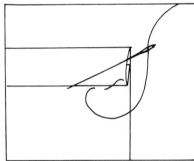

Figure 6

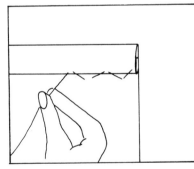

Figure 7

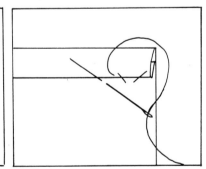

Figure 8

Basting

Basting, which can be done by hand or by machine, is a long, loose, temporary running stitch used to hold fabric in place, especially around curves and particularly important seams that you want to get just right. It involves the same principle as the running stitch, but in basting, take long stitches with short spaces in between. (Fig. 9.)

Figure 9

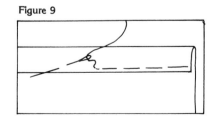

14

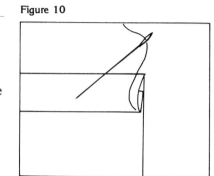

Whipstitch

The whipstitch (also called the hem stitch) is used for all types of hemming. Start with the thread pulled through just above the fold. (Fig. 10.) Insert the needle into the fabric immediately below the upper fold. (Fig. 11.) Bring the needle out just above the fold a little farther along; and pull the thread through being careful not to pucker your fabric. (Fig. 12.) Stitches should be about ¼ inch apart. (Fig. 13.)

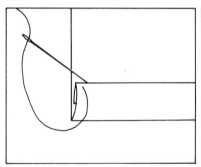

Figure 11

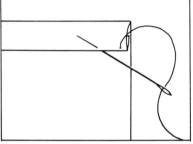

Figure 12

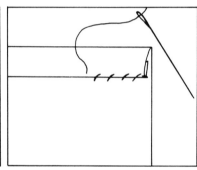

Figure 13

Blanket stitch

This stitch is used to attach thick woolen fabrics face to face without a hem, and, with variations, for embroidery. Unless you're using the stitch for decoration, all stitches should be about the same size. Insert the needle and thread under the fold or, if there is no fold, put the needle through the fabric and bring it up at the outer edge. (Fig. 14.) Insert the needle into the back of the fabric at the bottom edge of the fold so it is exactly underneath the first stitch. (Fig. 15.) While the needle is still half in and half out of the fabric, take hold of the thread near the eye of the needle and wind it once under the pointed end of the needle, from left to right. (Fig. 16.) Then, pull the thread right through, where it will be caught by a loop on the outer edge and, at the same time, will hold the edge down. (Fig. 17.) Decide how far apart you want the stitches to be, insert the needle and repeat the process. (Fig. 18.)

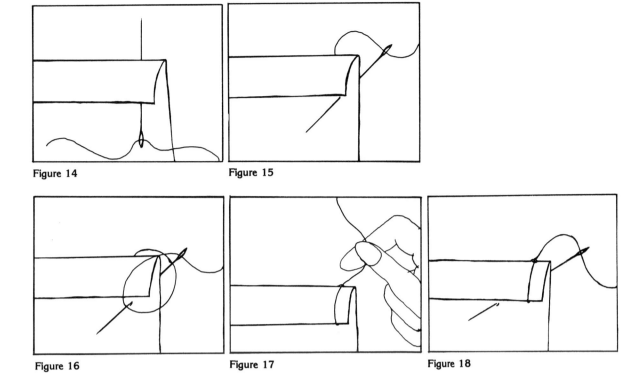

Figure 14   Figure 15

Figure 16   Figure 17   Figure 18

Backstitch

Backstitching has several uses and is a good substitute for machine stitching. To start, make a running stitch. (Fig. 19.) Insert the needle behind the thread at the end of the previous stitch. (Fig. 20.) Bring the needle out again, just in front of the thread. (Fig. 21.) Pull the entire length of thread through each time you make a stitch. (Fig. 22.)

Figure 19   Figure 20

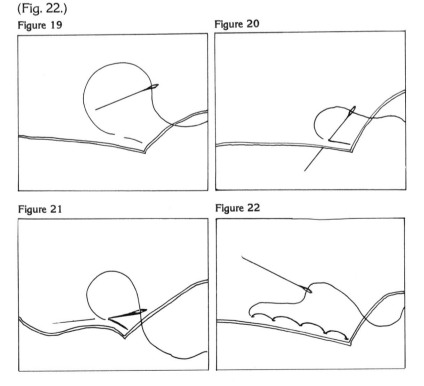

Figure 21   Figure 22

Blindstitch

The blindstitch is a machine stitch that is a standard feature on certain types of machines. It has the same effect as the hem or whipstitch. If your machine has this type of stitch, you will find that making hems is a real breeze.

Topstitch

The topstitch is not actually a type of stitch, but, since we use the term, we thought we might as well explain it here. Topstitching, as the name implies, involves stitching over something either by machine or by hand with a running stitch. It is used to finish seams, attach waistbands, and apply trim.

Zigzag Stitch

Certain swing-needle sewing machines can move from side to side as well as back and forth to produce zigzag stitching. This stitch is excellent for decorative topstitching and for finishing raw edges of materials that tend to unravel.

Seams

Seams are a method of joining two pieces of material together. They may be sewn by hand with a running stitch or by machine. Puckered, stretched, or wobbly seams will seriously detract from the appearance of your garment; so, take care, and don't be afraid to rip out seams and do them over until you get them right. If you do have to rip out a seam, use a pin, a seam ripper, or small scissors and clip every few stitches, pulling them out carefully from the other side of the fabric. Check the machine tension, pressure, and adjust the stitch regulator to suit the fabric texture and weight according to the directions in your sewing machine's instruction book.

All the seams in this book are to be sewn ½ inch from the edge. If you don't have a seam guide on your machine, make one by putting a small piece of colored tape ½ inch to the right of the needle hole.

Pin your fabric pieces together before sewing, placing the pins at right angles to the seamline with the heads toward the raw edges. This will keep the material from slipping while you're working and, in this position, the pins can be stitched over on most machines.

Seams are sewn on the wrong side of the fabric so that the right sides are facing. If for some reason you have to stop in the middle of a seam, start again 1½ inches farther back and sew on the original line to prevent gaping.

To begin a seam, start ½ inch from the end, backstitch to the end and stitch forward. To finish, stop stitching a stitch or two from the end of the fabric and backstitch for ½ inch. Clip threads. To make your seams lie flat, you will need to clip or slash the curves, being careful, of course, not to cut into the seamline. (Fig. 23.) When you've finished sewing your seams, you will either press the seam open or to one side, depending on what is required in the garment you're making. (Fig. 24.)

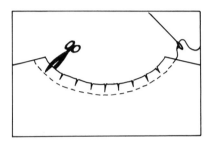

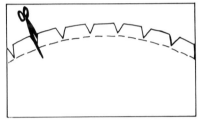

Figure 23

Hems

Hems are used to finish the bottom edges of sleeves, blouses, skirts, and dresses. We make our hems in one of two ways. The first way simply involves turning under ½ inch of fabric and pressing it flat. Then turn under another 1½ or 2 inches for sleeve seams, and sew it down using a whipstitch. The second method involves using hem or seam tape. There are two basic varieties of hem tape: stretch lace, which can be used on any type of fabric, and rayon tape, which can be used on any nonstretch fabric. Pin the tape to the raw edge to be hemmed, overlapping about ½ inch and topstitch. Fold under 2 inches and blindstitch by machine or whipstitch by hand. The type of hem you should make depends on the fabric you're using. Generally, very thin and very thick fabrics require the hem tape method, but ask your salesperson for advice. (Fig. 25.)

You can mark a hem by standing straight and still while the person marking the hem moves around you or, if you have no help, there are chalk markers designed to be used without help. After marking, turn the hem to the inside of the skirt, blouse, dress, sleeve, or whatever, along the hemline you have marked. Press along the fold. Use a ruler or hem gauge to mark an even distance from the folded edge all around and cut your hem to an even width. Finish the hem by one of the methods described above.

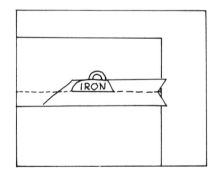

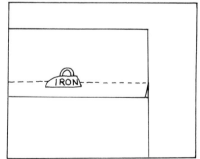

Figure 24

Gathering

Gathers are small, soft folds made by drawing fabric together on a line of hand or machine stitching. In order to have small even folds, you must get the right length stitch, not too long, not too short. A good rule of thumb is four stitches per inch. Thick and closely

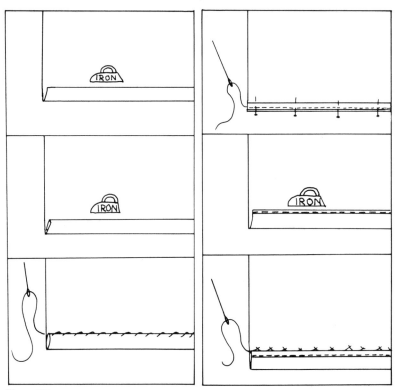

Figure 25

woven fabrics usually need longer stitches than lightweight and sheer fabrics. If the fabric doesn't gather easily, lengthen the stitch accordingly. If you're sewing by machine, silk or nylon bobbin thread will make it easier to pull up gathers without breaking the threads. The bobbin thread can be pulled more easily if the upper tension is loosened.

Start by stitching along the seamline on the right side of the fabric. Proper procedure is to then stitch a second line ¼ inch from the raw edge of the fabric, but we usually skip this step. If you are using a heavy, bulky fabric and have to gather across a vertical seam, stop when you come to the seam and start up again on the other side. If you are gathering by hand, use a small, even running stitch that is the same length on both sides of the fabric.

19

Secure the threads on one end by wrapping them around a pin and pull the threads on the other end to form the gathers. Now, adjust the gathers so that they are evenly spaced, secure the loose threads, and press the edges flat. (Fig. 26.)

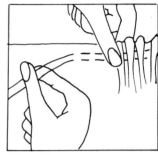

Figure 26

Pockets

Pockets can be both decorative and practical. Many of the garments in this book include an optional patch pocket. Patch pockets are sewn onto the outside of a garment, generally as a final step. They have square or rounded edges.

To make a patch pocket, decide what size pocket you would like and add 3 inches to the length and 1 inch to the width. Using heavy paper, make a pattern for your pocket. If you want a rounded rather than a square pocket, fold your pattern in half, draw an arc, and cut to round off the edges.

If you want two pockets, fold your fabric in half, pin your pattern in place and cut. If you only want one pocket, cut on a single layer of fabric.

Turn the top edge of the pocket under ½ inch, press flat. Turn under another 2 inches, press flat and topstitch as close to the edge as possible. Turn all other edges under ½ inch and press. Position pockets, using a ruler or yardstick to make sure they are properly and evenly spaced. Pin and baste them in place, and topstitch. (Fig. 27.)

Figure 27

Transferring designs

Even if you're terribly untalented when it comes to artistic matters, you can still produce lovely designs on your garments. If you are tracing an "actual size" design, all you need is a piece of tracing paper (paper that is thin enough to allow you to trace a design that some other, more talented, soul has already created). If you want to enlarge a design, first trace it on a piece of graph paper with ¼-inch squares. To make it twice as large, take a piece of graph paper with ½-inch squares and copy the design over square by square, just as you do when you are reproducing the patterns in this book. If you want to make the design half as large, transfer it onto graph paper that has eight squares to the inch.

Once you have your finished design on paper, you can trot off to your favorite fabric store and buy a dressmaker's wheel and carbon paper, which you will use to transfer the design to your T-shirt, dress, or whatever.

The sources for designs are endless. Needlework and other craft magazines often have wonderful designs that are already graphed out to be transferred. Any design or picture whose outlines stand out well can be used. One friend made a lovely T-shirt based on a Picasso print of a mother suckling a young babe. Any design you choose can be transferred to T-shirts, or any other garment for that matter, and then emphasized with trims, fabric print, crayons, marking pens, appliqué, or embroidery.

Trims

Commonly used trims include braid, ribbon, buttons, beads, and sequins. They can be used to outline designs, as borders, to add detail and texture to appliqués, and to emphasize major lines in your garment.

Braids, ribbons, lace edgings, and other trims can be sewn under edges or topstitched by hand (using a whipstitch) or by machine (straight or zigzag stitch). If the trim is narrow, one row of stitching down the center will hold it in place, but if it is wider, stitch it on both edges. If the trim has to be worked around a sharp corner, fold the trim back on itself and stitch on the diagonal. (Fig. 28.) Then, trim off the little triangle of excess so it will lie flat. Fold the trim down the other side and continue stitching.

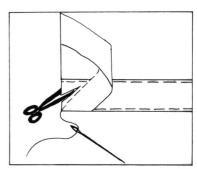

Figure 28

Beads and sequins must be sewn on with a strong double thread. Rubbing the thread with beeswax will prevent it from twisting and breaking. Ask the salesclerk in the fabric store to help you select the longer, more flexible, and finer type needles that are best for sewing on beads and sequins.

When sewing beads, select a thread that matches the color of your fabric. Beads can be sewn in two ways. To sew them on individually, use a backstitch, bringing the thread up from the underside of the fabric and through the bead; then, reinsert the needle a bead's length away from where it first came through the fabric. (Fig. 29.)

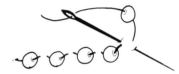

Figure 29

Or, you can string a row of beads on strong thread, then whipstitch the thread between each bead, securing it to the fabric. (Fig. 30.)

When sewing sequins, choose thread the same color as the sequins. To sew them singly, place a small bead on top of each to hold it in place; then, bring the thread up through each sequin and bead and back down through the sequin again. (Fig. 31.)

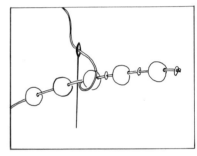

Figure 30

To sew sequins on in rows, bring the needle up through the center of the sequin and take a backstitch. Pull the thread through until the sequin is flat against the fabric. Continue in the same manner, overlapping the sequins. (Fig. 32.)

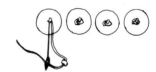

Figure 31

Appliqué   One of the easiest ways to personalize and specialize your wardrobe is to add an appliqué, which involves cutting various parts of your design out of material and sewing them onto your garment. You can create a scene, reproduce a design or, if you've got one, send a message to the world. However, remember that the fewer sharp lines you use, the easier your task will be. Fine lines will have to be done in embroidery or with waterproof markers or fabric paints.

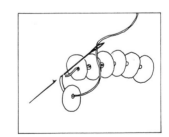

Figure 32

Appliqués can be either sewn on or ironed on. To make the sew-on kind, first decide on the design you want. Then, hunt through your scrap bag for appropriate pieces of material for each part of your design. Make patterns by cutting each piece of your design out of heavy paper. Pin your patterns to the fabric and cut, leaving an extra ¼-inch margin on all edges. Turn the edges under ¼ inch and press. Clip and slash at the corners if necessary.

Now you're ready to attach your fabric pieces to your garment. If you prefer, you can first trace the design on the garment with the dressmaker's wheel and carbon to make sure you get everything in the right place. Or, if you're the brave type, you can just "eyeball" it. In any case, pin the appliqué to your garment. It helps to quickly baste them in place before you sew them on, using the slipstitch, or, for a more decorative effect, the blanket stitch. If you have a machine with zigzag or other decorative stitches, you can use one of them to sew the pieces on.

A quicker method of appliqué is to cut your pieces out of iron-on fabric and bind them to the garment by pressing with a hot iron. Or, you can make fabric pieces as described above and bind them to the garment with a fusible web product, available in fabric stores, that allows you to simply iron the pieces on.

Painting or coloring on fabric
Once you've transferred your design to the fabric or have drawn it freehand with a fabric pencil, you can color it by one of three methods: waterproof marking pens, fabric paint, or fabric crayons.

Marking pens, the kind sold in art supply and stationery stores, come in a wide variety of colors. Make sure, however, that you choose pens that are labeled "permanent" or "waterproof" or your design will disappear in the wash. It's always a good idea to test the marker first on a fabric scrap. Pens don't work too well for covering large areas, but they're great for fine lines and small areas. They tend to fade after repeated laundering, but it's simple to touch them up. They're easy to work with, so easy that even a child can use them. In fact, if your expected child already has a sibling, get that child involved in decorating yours and the baby's T-shirts.

Fabric paints can be purchased in kits with a selection of colors or in larger containers in a wide range of single colors. Our favorite brand, Versatex, can be purchased in art supply and craft stores. The colors are much brighter and hold up much better than marking pens. Instructions come with all brands of these paints. Some of them require heat to set the colors. Use an iron, but be sure to cover the design with a piece of paper first. Remember to iron the wrong side of the design as well as the right side (some of the instructions omit this little tidbit).

Fabric crayons, which can be purchased in the same sorts of

places and also include directions, are excellent too. Some of these are used just like fabric paints, that is, the design is drawn on the fabric and then set with heat. Other types allow you to draw a design on paper and then transfer it to the fabric with an iron. Since the design is turned over in the process, it must be drawn in reverse. This is particularly important in motifs involving one-way designs or letters.

None of these materials is totally colorfast, but if you wash such garments in cold water with a mild detergent (never use bleach) and dry them on a flat surface without wringing them, you can avoid problems. If you need to press the garments, always use a press cloth between the iron and the fabric.

The following tips will help you in working with pens, paint, or crayons.
. Always wash garments before working designs on them; otherwise some of the design will wash off with the chemicals used in preparing the fabric.
. If you're working with a stretchy knit fabric — T-shirt material, for example — wear the garment a couple of times to stretch it out.
. Choose fabrics with smooth surfaces. Bumpy, textured, or straw fabrics take the paint, crayon, or marker lines unevenly.
. If you have a fabric that needs to be dry-cleaned, like silk, wool, and some synthetics, test the fabric on a hidden part (a seam or a scrap) to see how it takes the color.
. You can prevent the colors from soaking through from one side of your garment to the other by inserting a piece of cardboard between the layers of material. Pad this with folded newspapers to prevent the colors from spreading and bleeding back up to the surface you are working on.
. You may want to stretch the fabric ever so slightly over your cardboard and newspaper and secure it with pushpins to a solid surface like a piece of wood to give you a taut surface that won't bunch up as you draw with the crayons or pens.
. When ironing painted or certain crayoned areas, place a pad of press cloths between the fabric to prevent bleeding.

Embroidery   Another way of decorating your transferred designs is embroidery. Some of the stitches described earlier can be used for embroidery, but there are a number of other embroidery stitches as well.

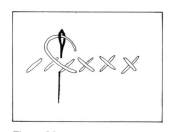

Figure 33

Cross-stitch

One of the most useful is the cross-stitch, which can be worked in either direction. If you start on the left, as shown in fig. 33, make a row of small diagonal stitches starting at lower left of stitch and going to upper right. At the end of the row go back over each diagonal stitch and cross it by going from lower right to upper left. Each cross-stitch can be worked separately also. All cross-stitches in a given piece will always cross in the same direction. (Fig. 33.)

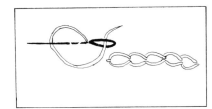

Figure 34

Chain Stitch

Another useful stitch is the chain stitch. To make a chain stitch, it's best to work from the top down. For the first stitch, bring the thread up through the fabric; insert the needle next to the thread and bring it out a short distance away. Be sure that the thread loops under the needle point. Pull the needle through. Continue working so that the stitches interlock. (Fig. 34.)

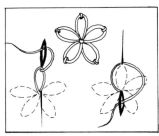

Figure 35

Lazy Daisy

The lazy daisy is a variation on the chain stitch. Begin as for the chain stitch, but instead of continuing with interlocking stitches, tie off each chain stitch by taking a tiny stitch at the top of the loop. Fan stitches around a centerpoint. (Fig. 35.)

Buttonhole Stitch

This stitch is used for hand-sewn buttonholes and as a decorative stitch. Bring the thread up through the fabric; make a vertical stitch a short distance away from the needle point coming out level with the up-coming thread; and pull it through, making sure the needle passes over the loop of the thread. Continue in the same manner. (Fig. 36.)

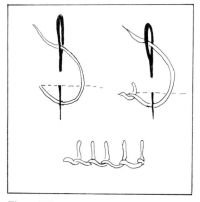

Figure 36

Stem Stitch

To make the stem stitch, which is useful for borders and edgings as well as flower stems, make a straight stitch; then bring the needle back out in the middle of that stitch. Pull the thread through. Continue in the same manner. Be consistent about holding the thread above or below the stitch being made. (Fig. 37.)

Satin Stitch

Another standard stitch, the satin stitch, can be used on the diagonal to create a leaflike effect or straight up and down to emphasize

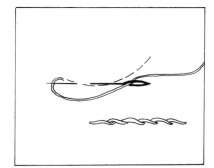

Figure 37

borders or fill in areas of your design. To start, bring the thread up; then, insert it a distance away and carry thread behind the work to bring the thread up in position for the next stitch. Stitches should be close together to make a smooth surface. (Fig. 38.)

Feather Stitch
The feather stitch is yet another of the basic embroidery stitches. Hold your fabric so that you can work from the top down. Draw a guideline to help you locate your stitches properly. Bring the needle up slightly to the left of guideline; hold the thread with your left thumb and, with the needle pointing out over the thread, make a slanting stitch on the right. Bring the needle out over the thread loop and, just slightly below, make a slanting stitch on the left with needle pointing to the right. Bring the needle out over the loop. (Fig. 39.)

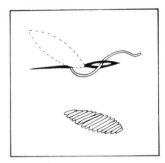

Figure 38

Now that you've learned all these fancy stitches, be creative. There is such an incredible rainbow of colors of embroidery floss available that you can hardly help but be inspired. Embroidery floss comes in varying thicknesses; ask the salesclerk to help you select the proper embroidery floss for your fabric. And, while you're at it, get her (or, more rarely, him) to suggest proper needles and to advise you about embroidery hoops.

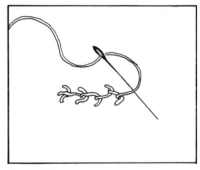

Figure 39

Dyeing

There are entire books written on the wonderful things you can do with a simple package of dye. So we'll just cover a few of the basics. The most important thing is the type of dye you use. We think you'll be disappointed with the type of dyes available in grocery stores. We use a commercial dye that produces good strong colors and doesn't fade. Our favorite is Fibrec, which can be purchased in good craft supply stores, some fabric shops, or ordered from the manufacturer (Fibrec, Box 14127, San Francisco, California 94114). The first time you wash a garment dyed with Fibrec, wash it separately; but after that you can throw it in with the other wash without worrying about the colors running. Don't, however, use bleach or enzyme products in your wash.

Instructions and useful idea booklets come with the dye, but these pointers will help you:

. Wash all garments to be dyed before dyeing to remove all the chemicals used to prepare fabrics.

. If you are color-matching two or more articles, such as a T-shirt and skirt, dye them at the same time.

. Although you can dye the fabric before you make your garment, it's better to wait until you're actually finished so that the thread is dyed at the same time.

We hope that our sewing tips haven't intimidated you. But, just in case, one last note: Nonsewers, novices, homemaking class flunkies, please take heart. You too can turn out wearable garments using this book. We know, because one of us is the four-thumbed idiot who failed Home Ec, was banished from Singer Sewing Classes for sewing the back piece of a pair of pants to the front of a skirt, and hasn't so much as sewn a button on in ten years. If she can do it, so can you. If you're still feeling timid, start with something like the Five-Minute Dress or the T-Shirt Halter Top from the Quickies section. In no time at all, you'll have a wearable garment *and* the confidence to go on to face greater challenges.

Remember, you're beautiful. Drape yourself in velvets and silks, put a jewel in your navel, have fun with this book, and send us a snapshot of the baby.

Basics

Kaftan

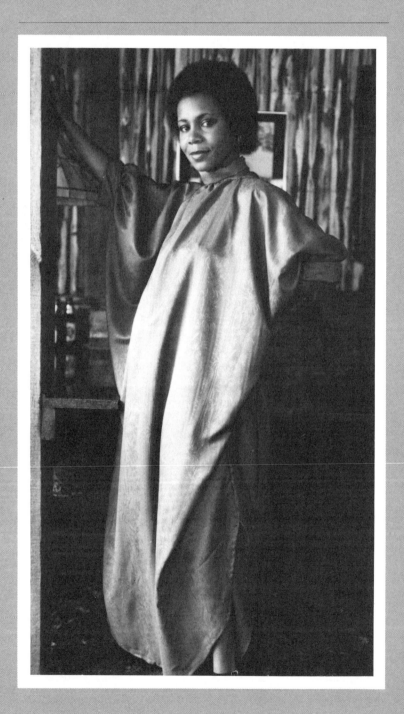

Materials   54-inch-wide fabric, length of fabric required depends on desired length of finished garment. ⅓ yard of facing material. Optional: ¼ yard for collar and cuffs; trims and closings.

The kaftan is probably the most versatile of our basic patterns and it's a snap to make. The kaftan can be worn as a blouse, a dress, or a floor-length gown, depending on how long you make it. It can also be opened all the way down the front to make a jacket, coat, or robe.

The fabric you select will alter the character of your kaftan. In terry cloth, it makes a comfortable robe or beach wrap; in Qiana, it becomes a sensuous, slinky dress; a silky material will transform this basic pattern into an elegant, flowing evening gown; a short version, made from a quilted fabric and closed with frogs (Oriental-type closings), can masquerade as a Mao jacket.

Our kaftan can be made in three basic shapes: rectangle, T-shape, or K-shape. (Fig. 41.) Full-length versions of the rectangle and T-shapes can be modified with tapered side seams. (Fig. 42.) All three versions can be made with a rounded hemline. (Fig. 43.)

The neckline can also be varied. It can be a simple horizontal slit or an oval to which you can add a vertical slit. The slit can be left open or closed with Chinese frogs, snaps, or looped buttons. You can also gather the oval and add a mandarin collar. A simple V-neck or square neckline works well too. These look especially nice when accented with trim. (Fig. 44.)

To determine how much material you will need, measure from your collarbone to the point where you want the finished garment to fall on your body. Double this measurement and add 6 inches for the hem allowance. Unless you are making the simple horizontal neckline, which doesn't require facing (which is a piece of fabric used to finish a curved edge so it lies nice and flat), you will need an additional ⅓ yard of fabric for facings. If you plan to add a collar and cuffs, you will need an additional ¼ yard of fabric.

Step 1   Decide what style kaftan you wish to make: its shape, length, neck, and sleeves. Fold your material in half crosswise, with right sides facing. Then, fold it in half lengthwise and mark the centerpoints

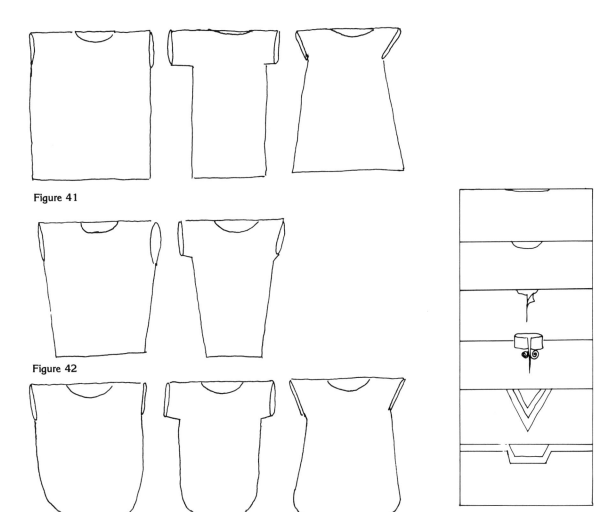

Figure 41

Figure 42

Figure 43

Figure 44

on the top and bottom edges. Unfold your fabric once, so that it is only folded crosswise, and mark two points (A and B), each 5 inches from the centerpoint, on the folded edge for your neck opening. Mark two more points (C and D), each 10 inches from the folded edge, on either side of your fabric for your armholes. (Fig. 45.)

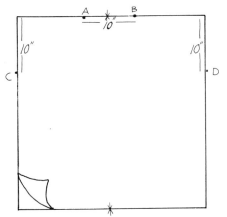

Figure 45

Step 2 Next, you will want to mark the cutting lines that will define the shape of the sleeves and body of your kaftan.

Rectangle
If you are making this version, you will not need to cut or mark the sleeves and sides.

T-shape
For this version, you will start at the lower armhole points (C and D) and draw a 10-inch line parallel to the folded edge of the fabric on either side to form your sleeves. Then, draw parallel lines from the inner end of these sleeve lines to the bottom of your fabric to define the body of your kaftan. If you are planning to make a full-length T-shaped kaftan and want to taper the sides, the sleeve lines should be 5 rather than 10 inches long.

K-shape
If you are making a K-shaped kaftan, mark two points on your fabric 15 inches from the folded edge and 10 inches from the outer edge on either side. Then, mark straight lines from these points to the lower armhole points (C and D) and to the bottom, outer edges of your fabric on either side. (Fig. 46.)

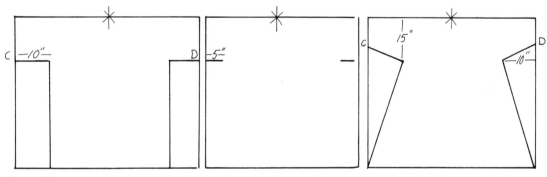

Figure 46

Step 3 If you are making a long kaftan and want to taper the side seams of the rectangle or T-shaped, you will need to mark those lines now; otherwise, you may skip this step. Find the centerpoint on the bottom edge of your fabric. Mark two points on that edge, each 14 inches from the centerpoint.

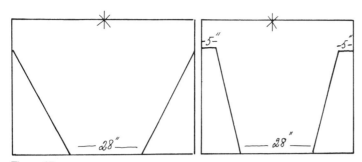

Figure 47

Rectangle

To taper the rectangle use a yardstick to draw a straight line connecting the points you have just marked on the bottom edge of your fabric to the lower armhole points (C and D) on either side.

T-shape

To taper the T-shape, draw a straight line from the points you have just marked on the bottom edge of your fabric to the inner point of your sleeve lines on either side. Remember that your sleeve lines will be 5 instead of 10 inches long on a tapered variation of the T-shape. (Fig. 47.)

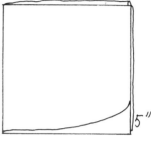

Step 4

If you want a rounded hemline, you will mark and cut that now; otherwise, you can skip this step. To round the hemline, fold your fabric in half lengthwise. Next, you will need to mark the high point of your hemline on the raw edges of the fabric. If you are making a full-length kaftan, mark a point on the raw edges that is 17 inches from the bottom edge of your fabric. If you are making a medium-length version, mark the point 10 inches from the bottom edge. For a short version, mark a point 5 inches from the bottom edge. Draw an arc from the centerpoint on the bottom edge to the point you have just marked on the raw edges. Cut along this arc to form your rounded hemline. (Fig. 48.)

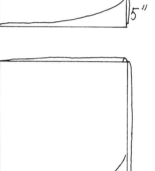

Step 5

Unless you are making a rounded hem, you will need to mark for kick pleats, which will allow for freedom of movement in your finished garment. For a full-length kaftan, you will want 14-inch kick pleats; for a knee- or midi-length, 7-inch kick pleats. Shorter versions that will be worn as blouses or jackets do not require kick pleats. To determine where to mark your kick pleats, decide which length pleat you will need and add 3 inches to that measurement to allow for the hem.

Rectangle

Measuring from the bottom edges of your fabric, mark points the appropriate number of inches from the bottom edge on both sides of your fabric.

T- and K-shape

Measuring from the bottom edges of your fabric along the cutting

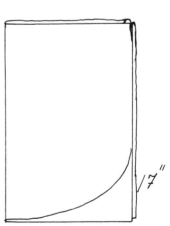

Figure 48

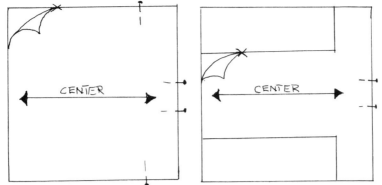

Figure 49

lines, mark points the appropriate number of inches from the bottom edge on the cutting lines on both sides. (Fig. 49.)

Step 6   Now you are ready to mark the neck opening.

Horizontal neck
For this version, the points you have already marked on either side
of the centerpoint on the top edge of your fabric (A and B) are all
you will need. Simply cut on the fold between those points to make
your neck opening.

Oval neck
If you want an oval neckline, mark a point 2 inches below the centerpoint on the top edge of your fabric. This will become the low
point of your oval. Using a piece of marking chalk or a fabric pencil, sweep an arc from this low point to points A and B as shown in
fig. 49. If you plan to add a collar or want a front opening, draw a
7-inch vertical line from the low point of your oval down the front of
your garment.

V-neck
For this version, mark a point 7 inches below the centerpoint. Draw
straight lines connecting that point with points A and B on the
folded edge.

Square neck
If you want a square neck, mark a point 7 inches below the centerpoint. Mark two points, each 4 inches on either side of that point
and parallel to the folded edge.

Use these points as a guide to draw an 8-inch line parallel to the
folded edge. Use a ruler to connect the endpoints of this line with
points A and B on the folded edge. (Fig. 50.)

Step 7   Cut your kaftan along the lines you have drawn. Note: If you're
making an oval, V-, or square neck, save the scraps you cut away;
you'll need them to make the facing. If you plan to open your kaftan down the front, mark a straight line between the centerpoints
on the top and bottom edges and cut the front piece of your garment along this line. Pin the garment on the sides and slip it on to

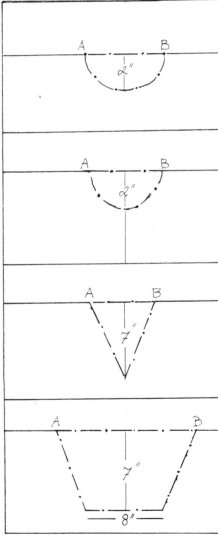

Figure 50

check the fit of the neck and width of the sleeves. Remove the garment and make any necessary adjustments. (Fig. 51.)

Step 8 Now you are ready to sew the side and/or sleeve seams.

Rectangle
Make a ½-inch seam on either side from the lower armhole points (C and D) to the kick pleat points. Press the seams open.

Figure 51

T- or K-shape
Make a ½-inch seam along the lower sleeve edges and the sides of the body to the kick pleat points. Clip the seams under the arms. Press seams open. (Fig. 52.)

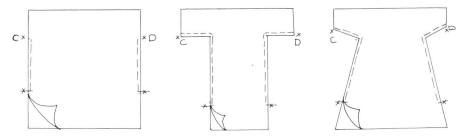

Figure 52

Step 9 Finish the edges of the kick pleats, armholes, and front opening, if you have one, by turning them under ¼ inch, pressing flat, turning under another ¼ inch, pressing again, and stitching. Or, you can sew hem tape on the raw edges, turn them under, and stitch down. If you are using a stretch fabric, you can simply turn your fabric under ½ inch and stitch since these fabrics won't unravel. (Note: If you are adding cuffs, it is not necessary to finish the armhole openings.) Make a hem along the bottom edge of the garment. (Fig. 53.)

Step 10 If you are adding a collar, go to Step Thirteen; otherwise, you will now need to finish the neck opening. The horizontal neck opening can be finished by the same method described in Step Nine. If you have added a vertical slit, the slit may now be finished in the same manner.

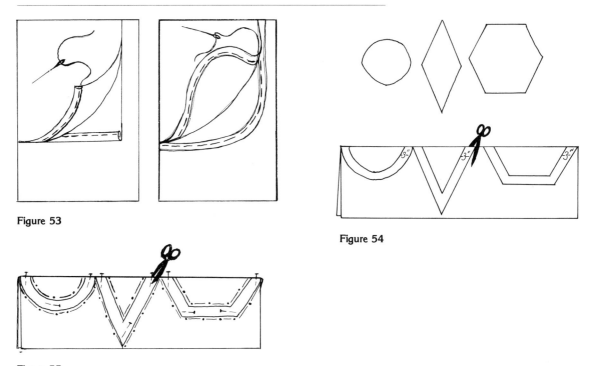

Figure 53

Figure 54

Figure 55

The other openings will require a facing in order to lie flat and look nice. The facing can be cut from any scraps of material. You can make the pattern for your neck facings using the pieces you cut away when making your neck openings. Simply fold the fabric piece that you have cut away in half lengthwise and lay it on a sheet of paper. Trace around the folded fabric piece, marking its outline on the paper. Then, measure a number of points, each 3 inches from the line you have just traced, around the fabric piece. Connect these points to form the outer edge of your pattern piece. Cut your pattern from the paper along the lines you have just drawn. (Fig. 54.)

Step 11   Fold your facing material in half lengthwise. Pin your pattern piece on the fold and cut. (Fig. 55.)

Step 12   Pin the facing to the kaftan, right sides facing, so the raw edges are even. Make a ½-inch seam all around the neck opening. Clip the

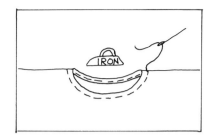
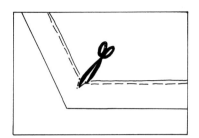

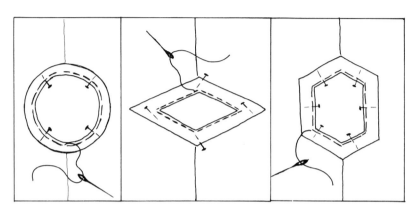

Figure 56

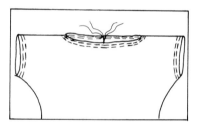

corners or curves and press the seam and facing toward the inside of the garment, hem the facing, and tack in place. (Fig. 56.)

Step 13 If you are planning to add a collar to your oval neckline with the vertical slit, gather the edge of your neck opening. (Fig. 57.)

Figure 57

Step 14 Cut a piece of material, 8 x 18 inches. Fold it in half lengthwise, right sides together, and make a ½-inch seam on each end. Turn right side out. (Fig. 58.)

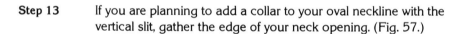
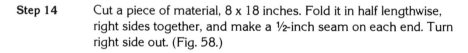
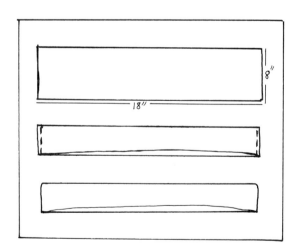

Figure 58

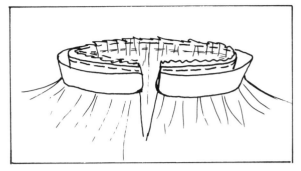

Figure 59

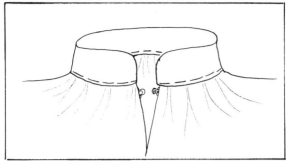

Figure 60

Step 15   Pin one edge of the collar piece to the gathered neckline so that the right sides of the fabric are facing and join with a ½-inch seam. (Fig. 59.)

Step 16   Turn your garment over so that you are working on the inside. Turn the unattached edge of your collar piece under ½ inch. Pin it to the inside of the gathered neckline. Baste and then slipstitch or topstitch in place. Attach a hook and eye to both inside edges to close your collar. (Fig. 60.)

Step 17   If you want to add cuffs, gather the edges of your sleeves. (Fig. 61.)

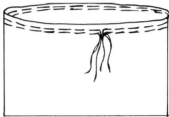

Figure 61

Figure 62

Figure 63

Step 18   Cut two pieces of fabric, each 5 x 14 inches. Form a circle out of each piece by pinning and stitching the ends of each piece of fabric with a ½-inch seam. Iron the seams open. (Fig. 62.)

Step 19   At this point, the easiest way to proceed is to turn the kaftan inside out and the cuff right-side out. Put the cuff inside the gathered sleeve and pin one of the raw edges of the cuff to the kaftan, adjusting the gathers evenly. Pin and baste. Stitch ½ inch from the edge. (Fig. 63.)

Step 20   Turn the remaining raw edge of cuff under ½ inch. Fold the cuff in half and stitch in place. (Fig. 64.)

Figure 64

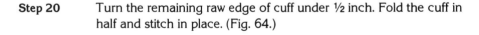

Wrap Dress

Materials   A length of 60-inch-wide stretch knit fabric, exact amount of fabric required depends on height: short (5 feet 3 inches and under); average (5 feet 4 inches to 5 feet 8 inches); tall (5 feet 9 inches and over) and size: small (8 to 10 pre-pregnancy size); medium (12, 14, 16 pre-pregnancy size). The following table will help you determine your needs:

Yardage Table

		small	medium/large
short	60″ fabric	2⅝	2⅝
average	60″ fabric	2⅞	2⅞
tall	60″ fabric	3⅛	3⅛

If you've spent most of your pregnancy schlepping around in oversized men's shirts and creations conceived by Omar-the-tent-maker, you owe it to yourself to make this dress. It could change the whole way you look at and think of yourself, for this very elegant dress hangs gracefully on a pregnant body. You can't help but enjoy yourself in it, especially if you make it up in a soft, sensuous, thigh-clinging material like Qiana. Even though at first glance it seems to be the kind of thing you'd wear when you're intent on dressing up for a special event, consider making one to wear around the house. After all, pregnancy itself is a rather special event.

This dress can be worn throughout the pregnancy for most women (although if you're germinating a ten-pounder, the last months might require a strategically placed pin), and afterward as well. The pattern and fabric requirements listed here are for a full-length dress, but it can also be worn with pants or skirts in shorter versions. A leotard (buy a size or two larger than normal) worn underneath adds warmth and versatility to this basic pattern.

This dress can be wrapped around your body in a number of different ways. We'll list our favorites, but fool around with it and you're bound to come up with some new ones of your own.

This one is probably the simplest. Place the seam in the center of

Figure 66

your back and lap the left front over the right. Bring the ties around to the back of your neck and tie into a bow. (Fig. 66.)

This knotted version looks a bit more exotic: Place the seam in the center of your back and lap the left front over the right. Wrap the left tie around the right tie to form a twist, leaving enough open to fit around your neck. Bring the ties around to the back of your neck and tie into a bow. (Fig. 67.)

Figure 67

Figure 68

This one is fancier still: Place the seam at center back and lap the
left front over the right. Wrap the left tie around the right tie to form
a twist. Cross the ties in back; bring them to the front, crossing
under bust; bring ties to back and knot. (Fig. 68.)

Figure 69

And this one is downright regal: Place the seam at center back and lap left front over right. Cross the ties in back; bring them to front; and tie into a bow under the bust. (Fig. 69.)

The only tricky thing about this pattern is the layout. Unlike the other patterns in this book, this one is cut from a single layer of fabric rather than a folded piece. This means that you will have to pin the pattern pieces on, cut pieces out, mark your fabric, and then remove the pattern pieces. Next, you will reverse the pattern pieces so that you are pinning them to the fabric with the right side of your pattern facing the fabric. Then, cut and mark again.

44

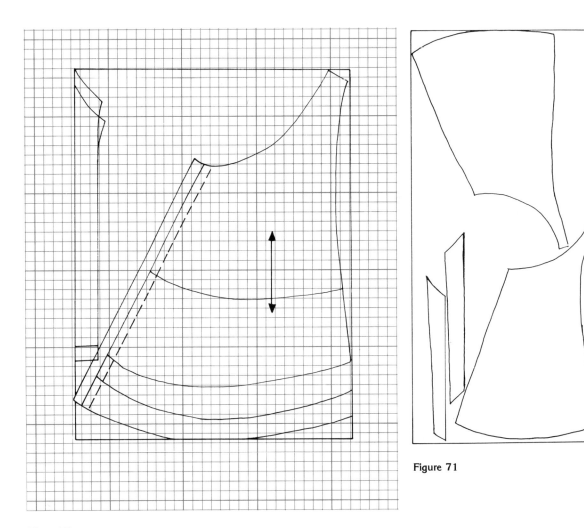

Figure 71

Figure 70

Step 1   Decide which size you will need and use the guide given here to make your own pattern. (Fig. 70.)

Step 2   Fold your material out flat. Pin the pattern pieces to the fabric according to the layout guide given here, cut, and mark. (Fig. 71.)

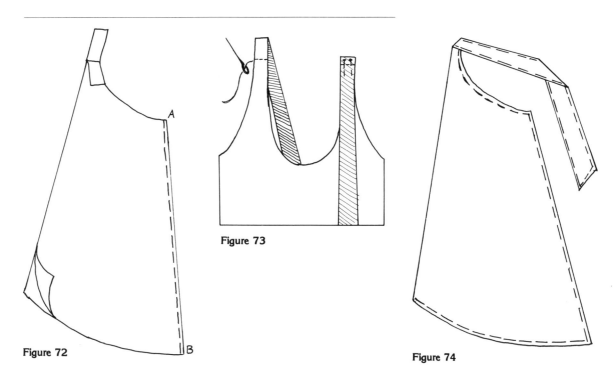

Figure 73

Figure 72

B

A

Figure 74

Step 3   Pin your dress pieces together, right sides facing. Join the pieces along the back (A to B) with a ½-inch seam. Because you are using a stretch fabric, you will need to seam a second time at ⅜ inch unless, of course, your machine has a zigzag stitch. (Fig. 72.)

Step 4   Next, pin each tie end to the shoulder straps. Join them with a ½-inch seam and, if you don't have a zigzag machine, stitch again at ⅜ inch. (Fig. 73.)

Step 5   You'll have plenty of time to practice your Lamaze breathing exercises while you finish the outer edges because it takes quite a while. Turn all edges under ½ inch and press or baste down. Stitch all the way around. Trim the seams. (Fig. 74.)

The Yoke

Materials A length of 54-inch-wide fabric, exact yardage depends on desired length of finished garment and sleeve options.

This pattern is a variation on the basic muumuu, a garment worn by countless women, pregnant and otherwise, in a wide variety of cultures. We call it the Yoke (in reference to its neckline) because we wanted to avoid the moo-moo-as-in-cow connotation and because it's cut a bit differently than the traditional muumuu: There is not as much material and it's not as full, so you won't feel like you're wearing a piece of camping equipment.

The Yoke can be made as a floor-length gown, a midi-length dress, a conventional-length dress, a three-quarter length tunic, a blouse, or a jacket, depending on your needs.

It can be made with or without sleeves to be worn as a sundresss, or with a turtleneck or jersey under it in cooler weather. The sleeves can be short, medium, long, or any length in between. They can be finished with a simple hem, a straight cuff or gathered with or without a cuff. (Fig. 76.)

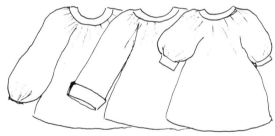

Figure 76

The yardage required will, of course, depend on which of these options you choose. To determine your yardage requirements, decide how long you want the finished garment to be. Measure from your collarbone to where you want the hem. Double this measurement and add 4 inches to allow for hem and seams. Then, measure the desired length of the sleeve and add 2½ inches to allow for hems and seams. If you want a cuff on your sleeve, you will need extra fabric. The rule of thumb for determining cuff yardage

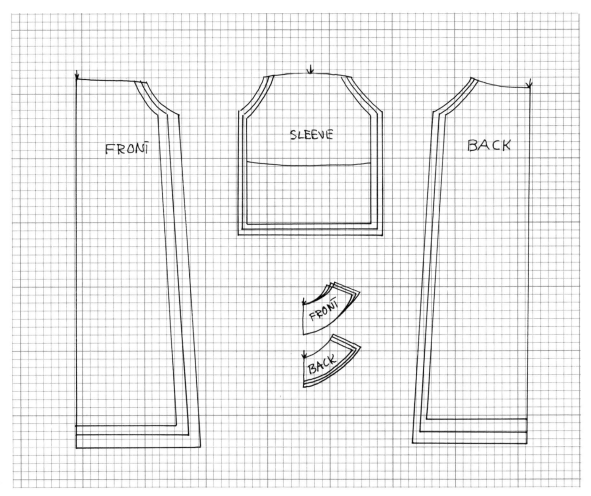

Figure 77

requirements is one and a half times the depth of the cuff equals fabric requirement. For instance, if you want a 2-inch cuff, you will need to buy 3 inches of extra fabric.

Since we've made a number of calculations here and probably confused you a bit, perhaps an example is in order. Let's say you're making a tunic-length Yoke top and that measuring from your collarbone to where you want the finished garment to fall (midthigh) gives you 24 inches. Double that to get 48 inches, add the 4-inch hem and seam allowance and you've got 52 inches. Next, let's say you want long sleeves and that measuring from your shoulder to your wrist, you get 22 inches. Since you are cutting on folded fabric, you will cut two sleeves at the same time so there is no need to double this measurement, just add 2½ inches for hem and seam allowance. So far you have 52 plus 22 plus 2½ which equals 76½ inches. Let's say you are adding a 2-inch cuff, which means an extra 3 inches, bringing the total yardage requirement to 79½ inches or approximately 2¼ yards of fabric.

The pattern guide given here indicates small, medium, and large sizes and will make a conventional-length dress with three-quarter-length sleeves on most people. If you want shorter or longer sleeves or body, simply adjust your pattern by shortening or extending the pattern guide. Pockets can be made from scraps of the same or contrasting materials.

As with all our basic patterns, the character of the Yoke depends on the choice of fabric. Almost anything from bright floral prints for a tropical effect to clinging blends or crisp cottons will do. Whatever you select, you'll find this garment comfortable and attractive.

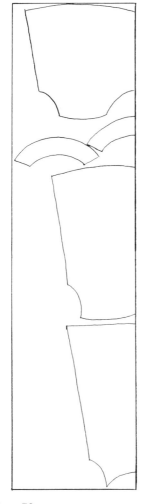

Figure 78

Step 1   Determine which size pattern you will need and what length body and sleeves you want. Adjust the pattern guide and make your own pattern. (Fig. 77.)

Step 2   Fold your material in half lengthwise and pin the pattern pieces in place. Mark the centerpoints on the top and bottom edges, and cut. (Fig. 78.)

Step 3   Take two of the four yoke pieces you have cut and lay them on top of each other, right sides facing. Pin and make ½-inch seams to join them together. Do the same thing with the two remaining yoke pieces. (Fig. 79.)

Step 4   Press the seams open. You should now have two circular pieces of fabric. Lay one on top of the other, right sides facing, and pin them

Figure 79

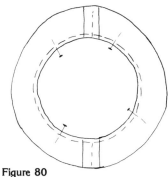

Figure 80

together. Stitch ½ inch from the inside edge (the small circle). Notch the seam. Turn right side out and press. (Fig. 80.)

Step 5 If you are planning to add sleeves, you will want to attach the sleeves to the body now. Pin sleeve points A and B to front piece of your dress along points A to B, right sides facing. Join with a ½-inch seam. Pin sleeve points C and D to points C and D on the back piece of your dress. Join with a ½-inch seam. Press the seams open and repeat the process with the other sleeve. If you are making a sleeveless version, finish the armhole edges with hem tape, turn the edge under, and stitch in place. (Fig. 81.)

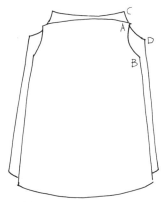

Figure 81

Step 6 Gather the top of the dress and sleeves, front and back. (Fig. 82.)

Step 7 Fold your yoke piece out so you are pinning only one of the edges of the large yoke circles to the gathered edge of dress and sleeves, with the right sides facing, being careful to match centerpoints. Adjust the gathers and baste in place. Then, stitch ½ inch from the edge, and press seam toward the yoke. (Fig. 83.)

Step 8 Hem the edge of the yoke and tack it down over the seam. (Fig. 84.)

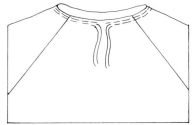

Figure 82

Step 9 Pin the lower sleeve (if you have sleeves) and side seams together and join with a ½-inch seam. Press seams open. (Fig. 85.)

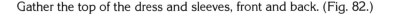
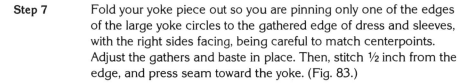
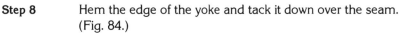
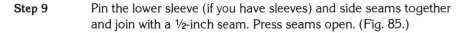

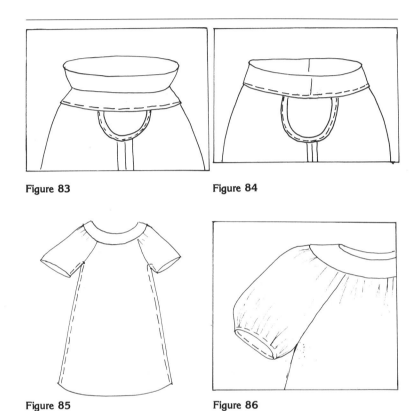

Figure 83

Figure 84

Figure 85

Figure 86

Step 10 Hem the lower edge of your sleeve. If you prefer, you may make gathered sleeves by turning under ½ inch, pressing flat, turning under another ½-inch, pressing again, and stitching on the folded edge. Leave a ½-inch opening so that you will be able to thread the elastic through the casing. Cut two pieces of ¼-inch elastic 1 inch longer than your wrist measurement. Thread through casing; secure with a few stitches; and slipstitch the opening closed. If you plan to add cuffs to your sleeves, see page 38 for instructions. (Fig. 86.)

Step 11 If you want to add pockets, do so now (for instructions, see page 19). Hem the bottom of your garment and that's it!

Gathered Skirt

| Materials | Two yards of fabric, width depends on desired length of skirt. ¾-inch waistband elastic, of a length equal to your waist measurement plus 10 inches; or a piece of fabric cord or braid, of a length equal to three times your waist measurement; or, if you prefer, you can make a drawstring from the same fabric. Optional: Ruffle and pockets, necessary yardage depends on depth of ruffle and size of pockets. |

This skirt is so simple to make that you could turn out an entire wardrobe of them in a single day. Once again the choice of fabric will define the character of the skirt. Hunt through your closet to find that old suit jacket whose pants or skirt have worn out. Choose a complementary fabric for your skirt and you've got a smart new suit. Or, use our favorite Qiana or any soft blend for a thigh-clinging, slithering garment that can be dressed up or down depending on what you choose for a top. Find some old 1930s drapery material or upholstery fabric and create a classic high-funk look. A batik fabric or Indian print will yield an ethnic look. Use a border print or calico for that down-home, country-peasant look. Our favorite version of this skirt was one we made in a border print. With the extra yard of material we bought by mistake, we made a shawl and created a striking outfit.

The length of the finished garment will depend on the width of the fabric you select and how tall you are. Thirty-six-inch-wide fabric will make a short- or midi-length skirt on most women; 45-inch-wide fabric will yield a midi- or full-length skirt; 54-inch-wide fabric will make a long skirt on anyone. To determine exactly where each width will fall on your body, use your tape measure. Subtract 4½ inches from that length (1½ inches for your casing and 3 inches for the hem allowance) to determine the length of the finished garment. If you are making a drawstring from the fabric, subtract an additional 2 inches. Of course, if you've fallen in love with a fabric that only comes in a 54-inch width, but you're only 5 feet 2 inches tall, you can always use the leftover fabric for a shawl or one of the scarfs described in the last section of the book.

You can also add pockets or a ruffle to your skirt. If you decide to add a ruffle, you will need extra fabric. The exact amount of extra yardage will depend on how deep you want the ruffle to be. Altogether, the strip of fabric you gather to make the ruffle will have to be approximately 4 yards long, but you can piece your ruffle together by cutting the fabric in strips and joining them together with a ½-inch seam. A yard of 36-inch-wide material, for instance, will neatly yield four 9-inch strips, each 1 yard long. You'll lose a couple of inches seaming them together, but you can easily adjust the gathers more loosely to accommodate this.

You have a choice of two waistbands, an elastic casing or drawstring. Either style can be worn across, over, or under the belly depending on your preference. Some women find anything across the belly annoying, whereas others find it comforting. If you are making the skirt in the early stages of your pregnancy, you might want to make an across-the-belly version that can later be worn over or under the belly. If you choose an elastic waistband to be worn across the belly, measure at your widest part, but leave an extra 10 inches of elastic that can be tucked inside the casing to allow for the alterations that might become necessary as you and your child grow. If you decide to make a drawstring waist, you can choose a fabric cord or braid for your drawstring, coordinated with the trim for your skirt perhaps, or you can make a drawstring from the same fabric that you've chosen for your skirt.

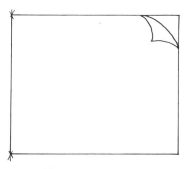

Figure 88

Step 1   Fold your fabric in half crosswise, right sides facing, and mark the centerpoints. If you are planning to make a drawstring from the fabric, cut a 2-inch strip off the top edge of your fabric. (Fig. 88.)

Step 2   Pin the fabric and make a ½-inch seam along the edge. Press the seam open. (Fig. 89.)

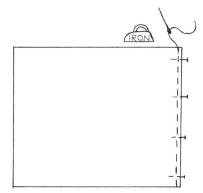

Figure 89

Step 3   To form the waistband casing, turn the top edge under ½ inch and press flat. Then, turn under another inch. Press and topstitch as close to the edge as possible, leaving a ½-inch opening in the back so that you can thread the elastic through the casing. If you are making a drawstring waist, leave the opening in the front and stitch on either side of the opening several times to reinforce. (Fig. 90.)

Step 4   If you are making an elastic waistband, thread the elastic in the proper place. Cut the elastic, adding an extra 10 inches so you can expand the waistline if necessary. Secure it with a few stitches. Tuck the excess elastic inside the casing and slipstitch closed.

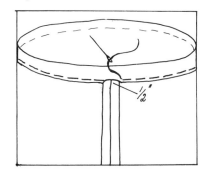

Figure 90

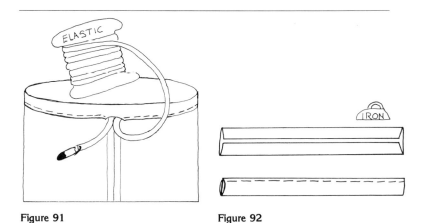

Figure 91   **Figure 92**

If you have chosen the drawstring waistband, thread your fabric cord through the casing and knot the ends so that the cord will not come loose in the wash. (Fig. 91.)

Step 5   If you want to make a drawstring from the same fabric, take the 2-inch strip of material, fold the long edges under ½ inch, and press flat. Fold in half, press again, and topstitch as close to the edge as possible. Tuck the ends inside and slipstitch closed. Thread through the casing and knot the ends. (Fig. 92.)

Step 6   Hem your skirt, and you're finished unless, of course, you want to add pockets or trims.

Optional   Decide how deep you want your ruffle to be. The piece of fabric from which you make the ruffle will have to be at least 4 yards long; however, you can piece this together by joining appropriate widths of material together, right sides facing, with a ½-inch seam until you have a strip 4 yards long. Fold this strip in half crosswise and mark the centerpoint. Join the ends of the strip with a ½-inch seam, press all seams open. Hem the bottom edge of the ruffle. Gather along the top edge and pull the gathers until you have a circle with a 2-yard perimeter; distribute the gathers evenly on either side of the centerpoint. Match the centerpoint of the ruffle to centerpoint of the skirt, right sides facing. You may want to pin extra carefully or baste so the gathers don't shift while you are working. Join the ruffle to the skirt with a ½-inch seam. Press the seam toward the skirt. (Fig. 93.) Voilà!

Figure 93

Pants

| Materials | A length of 36- or 45-inch-wide material, exact yardage depends on the desired length of the finished garment, and the style of waistband. Waistband elastic, if you choose an elasticized waist, of a length equal to your waist measurement plus 10 inches. |

This basic design can be dressed up or down according to your needs and wishes. The long version could be worn with a suit jacket for a tailored look. In a fine silky material, they could be worn with a flowing top for more dressy occasions. Or, made from terry cloth, they could be a casual pair of shorts. We've made these pants in cotton, velour, and Qiana and worn them everywhere from the grocery store to an evening on the town.

These pants only require one pattern piece, are easy to make, and once you've made your first pair, the next ones will be a breeze. They avoid the constricting panels found in most maternity pants, and we think you'll find them extremely comfortable.

This basic pattern can be cut to fit over, across, or under the belly. Some women prefer the over-the-belly version for reasons of warmth or modesty. If such considerations aren't important to you, we think you'll find the under-the-belly version more comfortable. And they can be worn after the baby comes as well. When preparing your pattern, remember that you will be cutting a bit differently depending on which version you choose.

The waistband on these pants can be made in three different ways. The easiest is the topstitched elastic. You will need to buy prefinished waistband elastic, which comes in a variety of widths and colors. The topstitched elastic waistband will not allow for as much expansion as some of the other waistbands. For this reason, it is particularly suited to the under-the-belly version, which won't require as much expansion as your pregnancy progresses.

If you prefer, you can make a casing and thread elastic through it. This is a bit more trouble, but allows for more growth and is suitable for the over-, across-, or under-the-belly versions. If you leave some extra elastic tucked inside the casing, you can always open it up and loosen the waistband if it gets uncomfortable later on. The waist can also be made with a drawstring, which allows for maximum expansion.

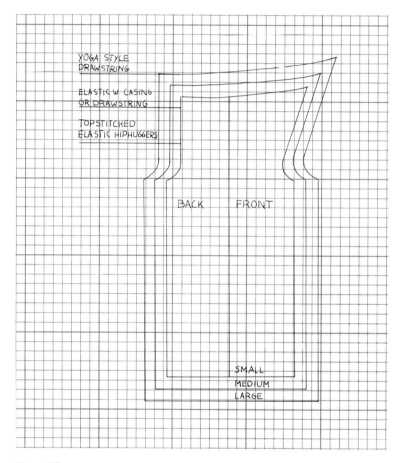

Figure 95

This basic pattern can also be cut to three different lengths to make shorts, knickers, or full-length pants.

You can further alter this basic design by changing the style of the leg openings. We've made several pairs with elastic in the legs so they become parachute pants. If you prefer, you can simply hem the bottom of the legs.

To determine the exact amount of material you will need to buy, measure from your waist (or where your waist used to be) to the desired length of the finished pants on your body. Double this

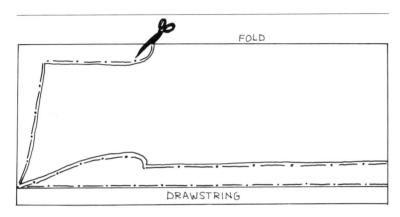

Figure 96

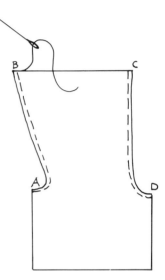

Figure 97

measurement and add 8 inches to allow for the hem and the waist-band. If you are making the over-the-belly version, you will need to buy an extra ¼ yard of material. If you want drawstring pants, add ⅛ yard of fabric to the amount you plan to buy to make the drawstring.

Step 1 Make the necessary measurements and, using the pattern guide given here, make your own pattern. (Fig. 95.)

Step 2 Fold your material in half lengthwise, right sides together. Pin your pattern piece to the fabric as indicated. (Fig. 96.)

Step 3 Cut your fabric according to the pattern. Now, carefully unpin and remove your pattern. Without moving the material, pin the crotch seams (A-B, C-D) together and join with a ½-inch seam. Clip the crotch and press the seams open. (Fig. 97.)

Step 4 Now fold the pants out. Pin and stitch the inside leg seams. Press the seams open. (Fig. 98.)

Step 5 Now you are ready to work on the waist. Turn the edge of the waist under ½ inch and press flat.

Topstitched Elastic Waistband
Sew the ends of your elastic together to form a circle that is comfortable for you to wear. Mark the centerpoints, front and back, of your elastic and match it to the front and back center seams. Pin

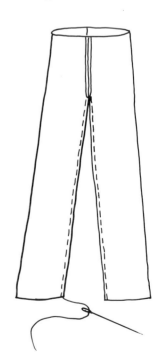

Figure 98

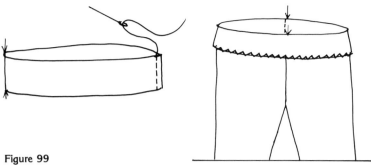

Figure 99

the wrong side of the elastic to right side of your fabric and top-stitch, stretching elastic to fit the fabric as you stitch. (Fig. 99.)

Elastic Casing Waistband
Fold the edge of your waist under 1 inch more and press flat. Top-stitch as close to the edge as possible, leaving a ½-inch opening at the back seam. Thread the elastic through the casing. Cut your elastic, leaving a few extra inches to allow for adjustments as you grow. Tuck the excess inside the casing. Secure with a few stitches and slipstitch the opening closed. (Fig. 100.)

Drawstring Waistband
Repeat the same steps as for the elastic casing, only leave your ½-inch opening at the front seam. Reinforce by topstitching ½ inch on either side of the opening. Cut a strip of fabric as indicated in the pattern for the drawstring. Turn the edges of the strip under ½ inch and press flat. Fold the strip in half, press, and topstitch along the edge. Tuck the ends inside and slipstitch closed. Thread the drawstring through the casing. Knot the ends of the drawstring to prevent them from working back through the casing in the wash. (Fig. 101.)

Figure 100

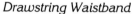

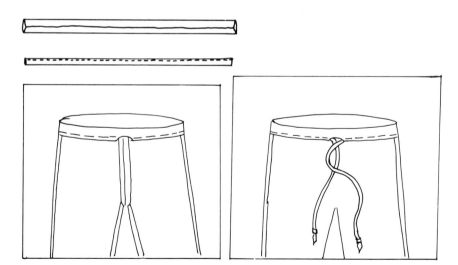

Figure 101

Step 6   If you plan to add pockets, do so now. You can finish these pants with a conventional hem or an elastic casing.

To make parachute pants, you will need to make an elastic casing just like the one you made for the waistband. Cut two lengths of elastic, equal to the length of your ankle measurement plus 1 inch. Thread the elastic through the casing. Secure with a few stitches and slipstitch the opening closed. (Fig. 102.)

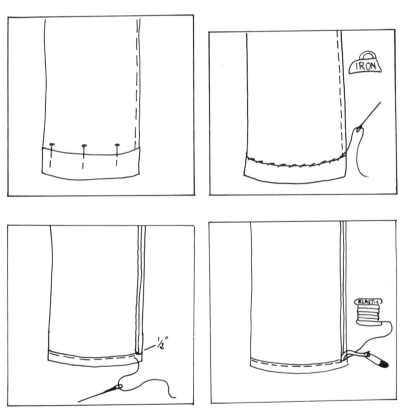

Figure 102

Cape

Figure 103   Figure 104   Figure 105

Materials   1 ⅔ yards of 54-inch-wide fabric. Optional: 4 ⅔ yards of trim.

This basic garment can be folded, wrapped, and wound around your body in a variety of different ways depending on your mood. We've figured out four different ways to wear this cape, and you'll probably be able to come up with some more.

For a tailored look, fold the cape as shown in Fig. 103; throw it around your shoulders and fold over the slits to form a collar and lapels. Pin closed with a brooch.

If you're feeling very romantic, try this face-framing version with a frilly peasant blouse and skirt. Fold the cape as shown in Fig. 104, drape it around your head and shoulders, and wrap in front. Or, if you need to be a bitmore practical, fold the same way and slip your arms through the slits to make a comfortable short version (Fig. 105).

The character of your chameleon cape can also be changed by your choice of fabric. It works very well when cut from a heavy blanket. Not only is it warm and comfy, bwon't even have to worry about finishing the edges. Coordinate it with the fabrics you've chosen for your basic skirts or pants, and wear it in our tailored version, and you've got a suit. Make one to go with your basic wrap dress, or for that matter with just about any garment in this book.

Step 1   Decide which size cape you want to make and select the proper arm slits. Using the guide given here, make your pattern. (Fig. 106.)

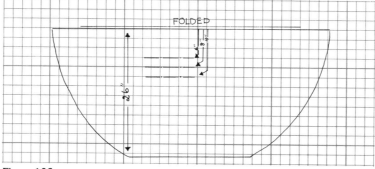

Figure 106

Step 2   Fold your fabric in half crosswise, right sides facing. Pin your pattern in place and cut. (Fig. 107.)

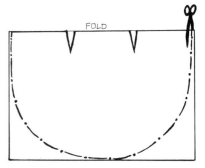

Step 3   If you are using a blanket, you may be able to get away without finishing the armholes, since usually the fabric will not unravel. Otherwise, to finish the edges, bind them with seam tape, then press and topstitch. Of course, if you are using a stretch fabric, you can simply turn under ½ inch and topstitch. (Fig. 108.)

Step 4   If the outside edges are not finished, you will need to do that next. If you are using a stretch fabric, turn under ½ inch and topstitch, or, with other fabrics, finish the edge with seam tape, then turn under ½ inch, press flat, and topstitch in place. If you want to add braid, or some other sort of premade trim, simply pin it in place and topstitch. If you plan to add pockets, do so now. (Fig. 109.)

Figure 107

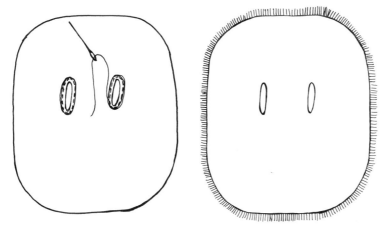

Figure 108   Figure 109

Quickies

Five-Minute Dress

Materials   A length of commercially shirred dress material equal to your bust measurement less 6 inches. 1½ yards of ribbon or other strap material or ¼ yard of fabric for making straps.

One seam, two straps, and a hem and you've made the dress pictured here. Wear it with a turtleneck jersey in cool weather and as a sundress in warm weather. Or, make a shorter version to wear as a top with skirts and pants.

The real timesaver is, of course, the shirred or pregathered material that comes on bolts and can be purchased at any good fabric store. It is sold by the inch, and prices vary according to the type of fabric. It is available in cotton blends and in heavier fabrics. Recently, it has become available in tiered ruffles. The dress fabric has about 6 inches of shirring and comes in different lengths, some of it prehemmed. It is also available with a 2-inch shirring, but the 2-inch does not hang as well on a pregnant body. In order to determine how much material to buy, take your bust measurement at the fullest part and subtract 6 inches.

You can find all sorts of unusual strap materials: ribbons, cotton rope, trims, and so on, in the notions section of your fabric store. Decide which style of strap you prefer: over-the-shoulder, criss-cross-in-the-back, or tie-behind-the-neck. Use your tape measure to determine how much strap material to buy, adding a couple of inches to allow for seaming. (Fig. 111.)

Figure 111

Some manufacturers make ready-made strap material to go with their shirred materials, or you can buy an extra ¼ yard of fabric and make your own straps.

Step 1   Fold your fabric lengthwise, right sides together. Pin and stitch a seam ½ inch from the edges. (Fig. 112.)

Step 2   If you are using premade straps, simply cut them to the proper length and secure to the dress with a few stitches. If you are making your own straps, cut two strips from the length of strap fabric. The strips should be twice as wide as you want the finished straps to be. The length of the straps will depend on which style strap you are making. Fold each strip in half lengthwise and crease with an iron. Fold out flat and fold both edges toward the crease. Press flat. Fold in half, press again, and topstitch. Tuck the ends inside and slipstitch closed. Secure to the dress with a few stitches. (Fig. 113.)

Step 3   Many of the shirred materials come prehemmed; but, if yours isn't or, if you don't like the length, simply hem the bottom and you've got a new dress to wear. (Fig. 114.)

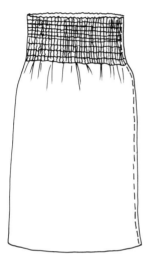

Figure 112

Figure 113

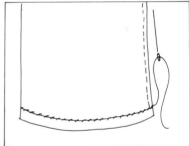

Figure 114

Shoulder-Tie Dress

Materials   1 ¾ yards of 45-inch-wide fabric.

Here again, we've made a full-length version of this pattern and worn it as a dress, but a shorter version could be worn with pants or skirts. It can be worn by itself as a sundress or over a turtleneck jersey as a jumper.

The dress ties at the shoulder by means of two straps that are run through a casing at the top of the dress, front and back. You can adjust the length of the dress somewhat by simply loosening and tightening the straps.

You should be able to wear this garment throughout the nine months of your pregnancy, no matter how big you get. It can accommodate a 59-inch belly and you couldn't possibly get bigger than that, could you?

Step 1   Cut your fabric according to the pattern guide. (Fig. 116.)

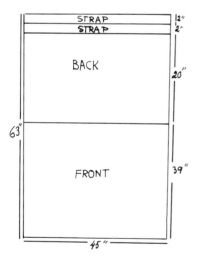

Figure 116

Step 2   Pin the front and back pieces together with the right sides of the fabric facing. You will notice that the front piece is larger than the back piece. Slip the dress on and mark approximately where you want the hem to fall. Remove the dress and mark points 6 to 10 inches from the hemline on either side for your kick pleats. Mark points 6 inches from the top edge on either side of your armholes. (Fig. 117.)

Step 3   Make a seam ½ inch from the edge on both sides from the armhole point to the kick pleat slit point. (Fig. 118.)

Step 4   Finish the armholes and kick pleats by turning the raw edges under ¼ inch and ironing them flat. Fold the edges under another ¼ inch; iron flat and topstitch. (Fig. 119.)

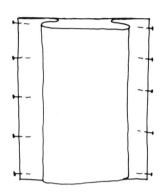

Figure 117

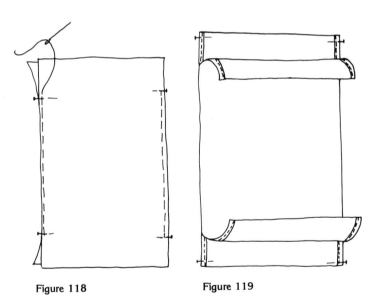

Figure 118   Figure 119

Step 5   To make the casing for your ties, turn the top edges, front and back, under ½ inch and iron flat. Fold under another 1 inch, iron, and stitch along the bottom edge. (Fig. 120.)

Step 6   To make the straps, fold your pieces of strap fabric in half lengthwise, right sides facing. Iron flat and make a ½-inch seam. Trim the

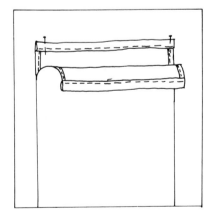

Figure 120

seams and turn the straps right side out. Tuck the raw edges in and slipstitch closed. (Fig. 121.)

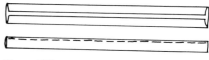

Figure 121

Step 7   Use a safety pin to thread the straps through the casing. Slip the garment on, adjusting the straps, and mark the final hem. Then, take the garment off and hem it. Put it back on and admire your finished product. (Fig. 122.)

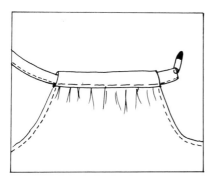

Figure 122

Kimono

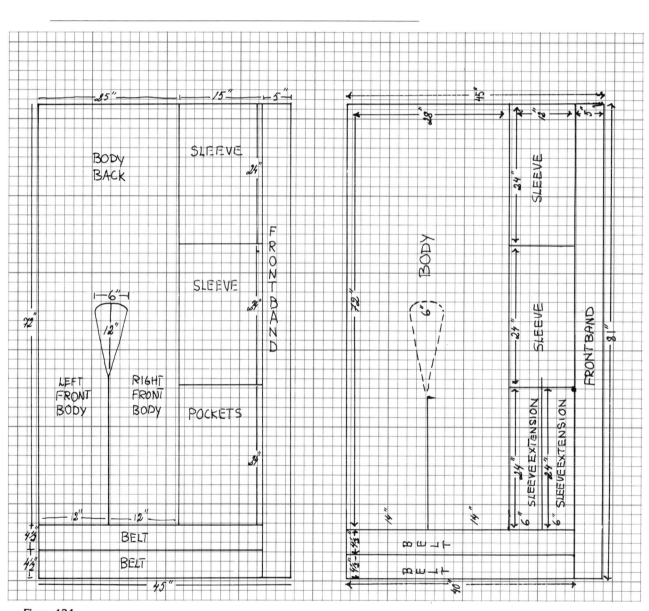

Figure 124

Materials	2¼ yards of 45-inch-wide fabric.

The kimono is so comfortable that it will probably become one of your favorite garments. It can be made in a wide variety of fabrics and, depending on which fabric you choose, can be worn for almost any occasion. It can be worn after pregnancy as well and is particularly convenient for nursing.

The pattern guide given here will make a kimono that falls somewhere between midthigh and midcalf depending on how tall you are. You can determine where the finished garment would fall by measuring on your own body. Since the entire body portion measures 72 inches, measuring half that distance, 36 inches, from your shoulder down the length of your body and subtracting 3 inches for the hem will show you exactly how long your kimono will be.

If you want a longer kimono, you can simply extend the pattern given here. Remember that you will have to move the neck opening and extend the front opening as well. For instance, if you wanted to add 10 inches to the length of your kimono, you would need an extra 20 inches of fabric. Then, you would extend the pattern guide 20 inches in the body of the kimono (not in the sleeves or other pattern parts though). Move the neck opening up 10 inches and extend the front opening 10 inches as well. For a shorter kimono, you will have to move the neck opening down and shorten the front opening.

Step 1 Decide which size kimono you will need to make; using the pattern guide given here, make and mark your own pattern. (Fig. 124.)

Step 2 Pin your pattern to your fabric, make the necessary markings, and cut the main pattern pieces and front openings. (Fig. 125.)

Step 3 Take your front band piece, fold it in half crosswise, and mark the centerpoints. Match the centerpoint of the band to the centerback of the neck. Pin the raw edge of the band to the kimono body, right sides facing, all around the neck and front edges. (Fig. 126.)

Step 4 Baste the band to the kimono. This basting step is necessary since this is the major line of the garment and you want it to be smooth and lie flat. Then, seam ½ inch from the edge. (Fig. 127.)

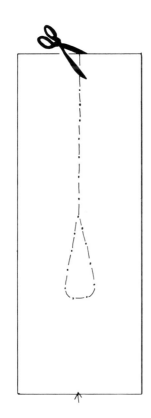

Figure 125

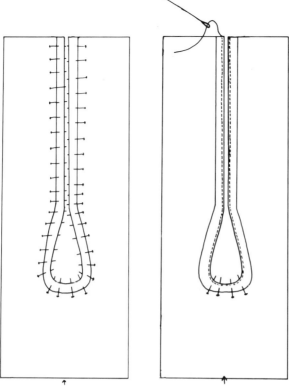

Figure 126   Figure 127

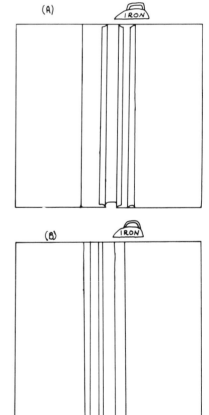

Figure 128

Step 5   Turn the edges of the band under ½ inch and press flat. Fold the band in half and press again. (Fig. 128.)

Step 6   Press band toward the opening of the kimono as shown here. Top-stitch as close to the edge as possible. (Fig. 129.)

Step 7   Mark the centerpoint on your sleeve pieces. Lay the sleeves on the kimono so that the right sides are facing and the centerpoints are aligned. (Fig. 130.)

Step 8   Pin the lower sleeve and sides together and join with a ½-inch seam. Slash the underarms and iron seams open. (Fig. 131.)

Step 9   Hem the lower edge and sleeves either by attaching seam tape and turning under or by turning under twice, pressing, and stitching, whichever is appropriate for the fabric you are using. (Fig. 132.)

Step 10   Join your two pieces of belt fabric together with a ½-inch seam. Iron the seam open. Fold the belt in half lengthwise, right sides facing. Stitch ½ inch from the edges; turn right side out; tuck the raw edges in and slipstitch closed. (Fig. 133.)

Optional If you want to add pockets, do so now.

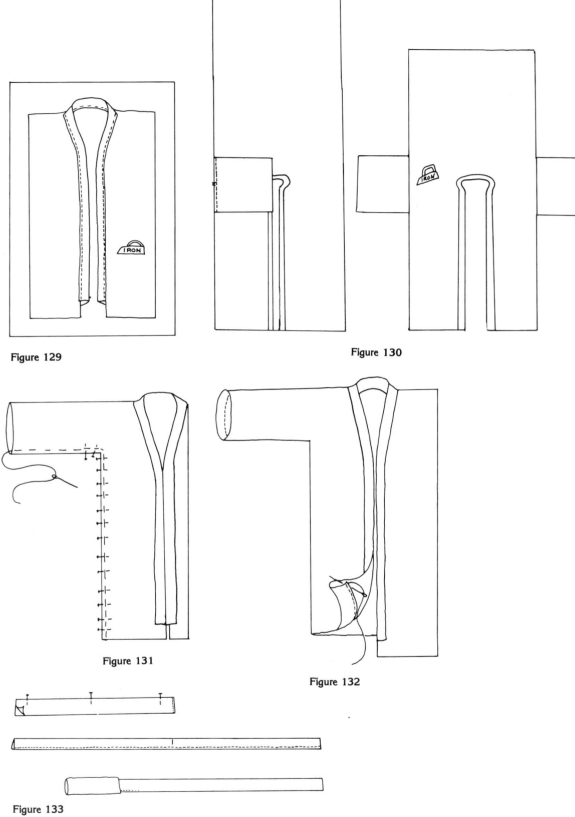

Figure 129

Figure 130

Figure 131

Figure 132

Figure 133

Dhoti Pants

Materials   36-inch fabric, amount of fabric equal to twice the desired length of finished garment; 4 yards of 1-inch-wide ribbon or braid.

These Indian pants may look a bit strange, but people are already staring at you so why not give them something really odd to look at. We made a pair from Qiana, so the material fell in soft folds. Since we used Qiana, we didn't bother about finishing the selvage edges, which get lost in the folds anyhow. However, if you're a perfectionist, you could turn the raw edges under once or twice, depending on your fabric, and topstitch.

To determine the length of fabric you will need, measure from your waist to the desired length on your body, and double that figure. Before you start to work with your fabric, you will need to make sure your material is cut in a straight line so the pants will hang properly. As we mentioned in the Introduction, this is called evening the material. To make sure that you really have a straight edge, pull one of the cross threads on the raw edge of the fabric. It will come off easily if the fabric has a true edge.

Step 1   Fold the top and bottom raw edges of your material over ½ inch so the right sides of the fabric are facing. (No, this isn't a misprint. Even though every other edge that is turned under in this book results in the wrong side of the fabric facing, we do want you to turn it under the opposite way this time. That way, once the ribbon is applied, your raw edges will be completely finished.) Gather the folded edge. (Fig. 135.)

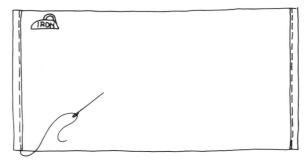

Figure 135

Step 2   Cut your ribbon in two equal pieces. Center each piece of ribbon over the edges you have just turned under and gathered. Pin in place. Topstitch on the upper and bottom edges, as close to the edge as possible. (Fig. 136.)

Step 3   Cut the ends of the ribbon on the diagonal so the ribbon won't unravel, and your pants are ready to wear. (Fig. 137.)

Figure 136

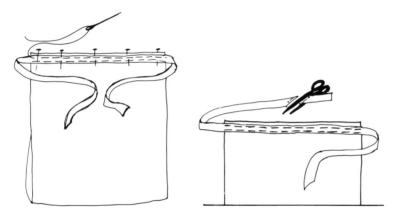

Figure 137

Pareu

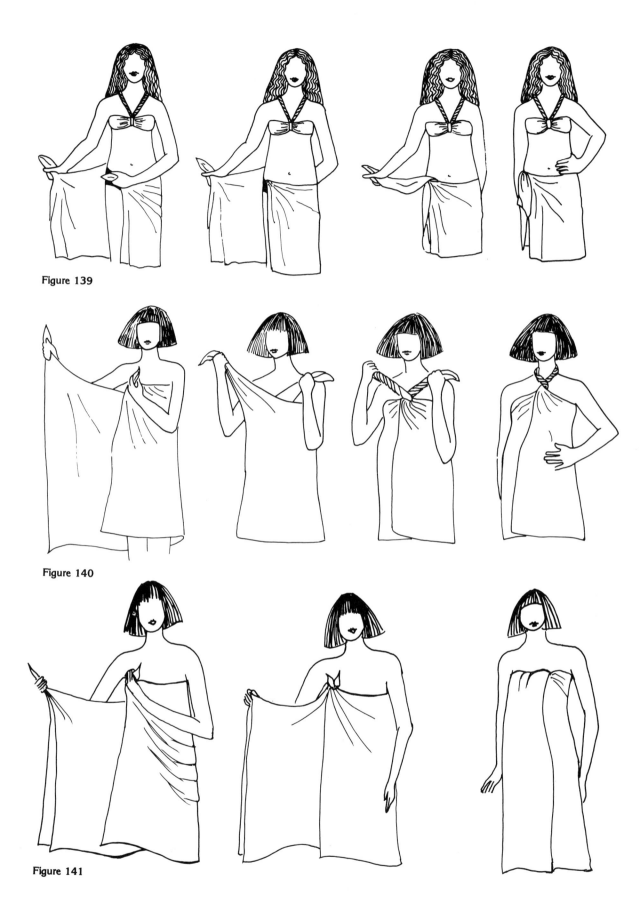

Figure 139

Figure 140

Figure 141

Materials	A length of fabric: 35 x 72 inches for the short version, and 45 x 72 inches for the longer ones. Optional: a large square scarf or long rectangular scarf.

You may find that your pareu gets a little skimpy in your last months. A strategically placed pin can help. Since you haven't cut the fabric or sewn a stitch, it's no great tragedy if you outgrow your pareu.

The pareu is one of the simplest bathing suit cover-ups around and also looks great with one of the halter wraps described in the next section. With the right choice of fabric and accessories, you could even wrap yourself up for a night on the town.

The short pareu	Fold your fabric in half lengthwise. Wrap the fabric around your hips with the fold at the top and shift slightly so you have one long and one short end. Then, make a knot with the short piece and a section of the folded edge from the long piece. Next, take the remaining portion of the long end, pass it under the knot, pull about 12 inches through, and fan it out. (Fig. 139.)
The halter wrap	Fold your cloth in half lengthwise. Wrap the scarf around your back with the two ends stretching out in front of you. Hold the ends out stiffly and cross the two pieces tightly. Twist the ends around each other and knot behind your neck. (Fig. 140.)
Bustline/ hipline wrap	Place the pareu around your back at your bustline or hipline so that the ends are front and center. Shift the fabric slightly so you have a long and short end. Take the end of your short piece and a section of the top edge and make a good tight knot close to your under-arm and tuck under. Take the remaining material and fold it twice to form the front panel. Tuck the edges of the panel under. (Fig. 141.)
Optional	For extra flair, take a large square scarf, fold it into a triangle, and tie around your hips Gypsy style. Or take a super-long (7-foot) scarf, drape it around your hips and knot dead center. For a really fancy version, twist two 6- to 7-foot chiffon scarfs into ropes and knot together on the side of the hips. (Fig. 142.)

Figure 142

Hooded Robe

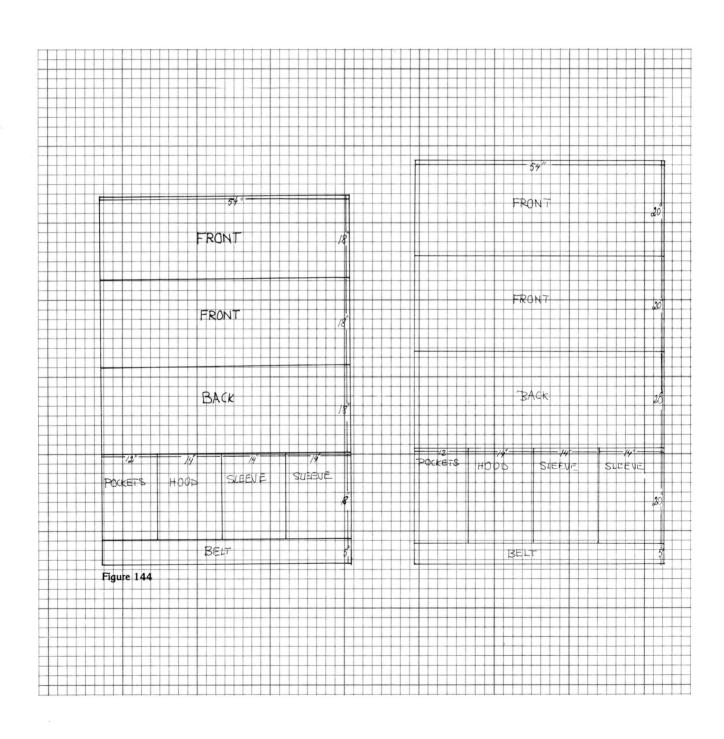

Figure 144

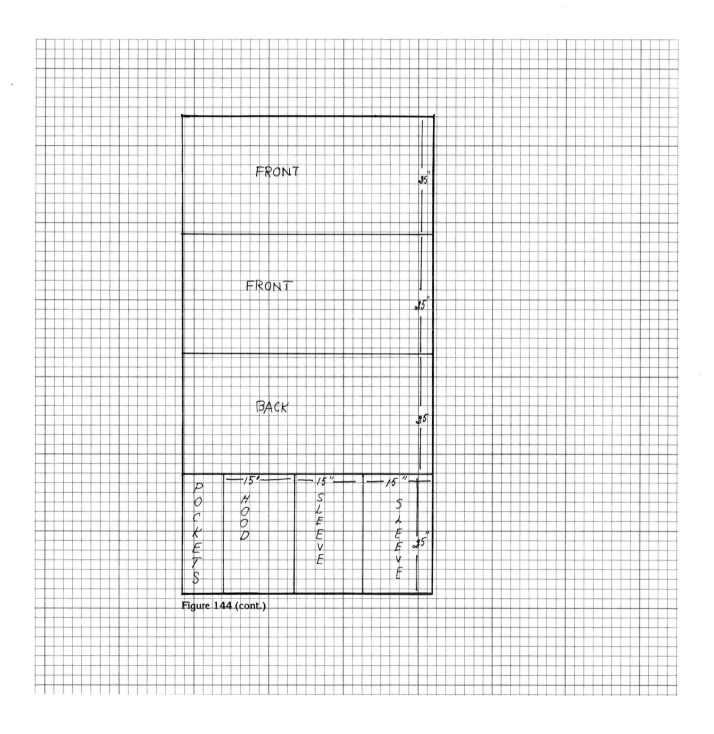

Figure 144 (cont.)

Materials	A length of 54-inch-wide fabric: 2¼ yards for a small-size; 2⅓ yards for a medium-size; and 3 yards for a large-size robe.

This one's so simple that you won't even have to make a pattern. If you make it out of stretch terry or cotton velour, it makes a great robe. Or, if you use a heavy blanket, bonded wool, or upholstery or drapery fabric, it makes a great coat. The version we've made here is a long one that should fall somewhere between midcalf and floor-length depending on your height. A shorter version, though, would make a great jacket.

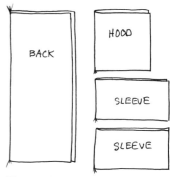

Figure 145

Step 1 Decide which size garment you will need, mark, and cut your fabric according to the guide given here. (Fig. 144.)

Step 2 Fold your back piece in half lengthwise and mark the centerpoints. Fold your sleeve pieces and hood pieces in half crosswise and mark the centerpoints. (Fig. 145.)

Step 3 Lay the back piece out, right-side up. Lay the right and left front pieces on top of the back piece so that right sides are facing and the outer edges of the garment are even. Since the front pieces are wider than the back piece, you will have some overlap. (Fig. 146.)

Step 4 To form the shoulder seam of your garment, pin and make a ½-inch seam from points A to B and D to C. (Fig. 147.)

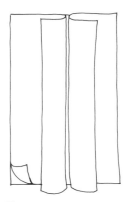

Figure 146

Step 5 Open your garment out so the right sides are facing you. Pin your sleeves to the garment, right sides facing, making sure the centerpoint of your sleeve pieces match the shoulder seam. Join the sleeves to the body with a ½-inch seam. (Fig. 148.)

Step 6 Open the sleeves out and press them flat, making sure that you press the seam toward the sleeve. (Fig. 149.)

Step 7 Fold your hood piece in half crosswise so the right sides are facing and make a ½-inch seam on one edge (not on the edge opposite the fold) to close the top of your hood. (Fig. 150.)

Step 8 Match the back centerpoint of your hood to the point where all three pieces of the body come together. Pin the remaining edges of the front pieces to either side of the hood and join them together with a ½-inch seam. (Fig. 151.)

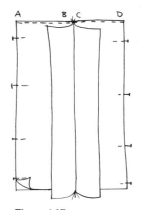

Figure 147

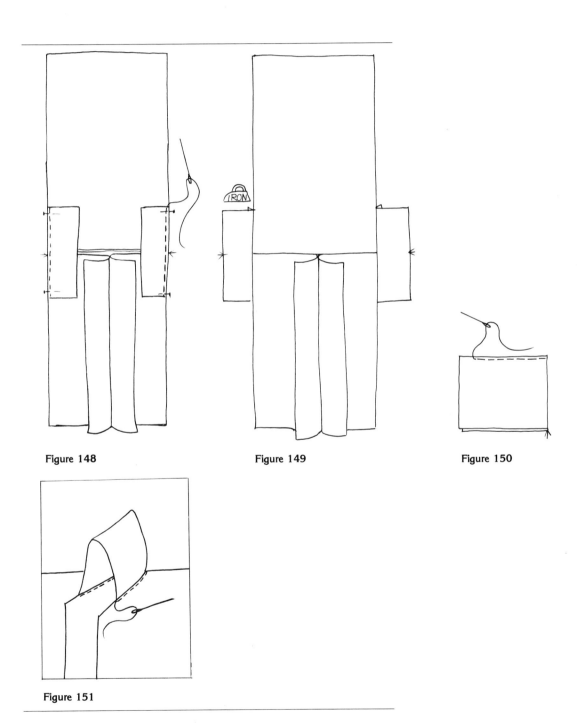

Figure 148

Figure 149

Figure 150

Figure 151

Step 9   Pin the lower sleeve edges and sides of the body, front and back, together and join with a ½-inch seam. (Fig. 152.)

Step 10   Hem the edges of the front opening and the edges of the hood by turning the raw edges under ½ inch, pressing flat, then turning under another inch, pressing flat, and topstitching as close to the edge as possible.

Step 11   Fold your belt piece in half lengthwise and press. Fold out flat and fold both edges toward the crease. Press flat. Fold in half, press again, and topstitch as close to the edge as possible. Tuck the ends inside and slipstitch closed. (Fig. 153.)

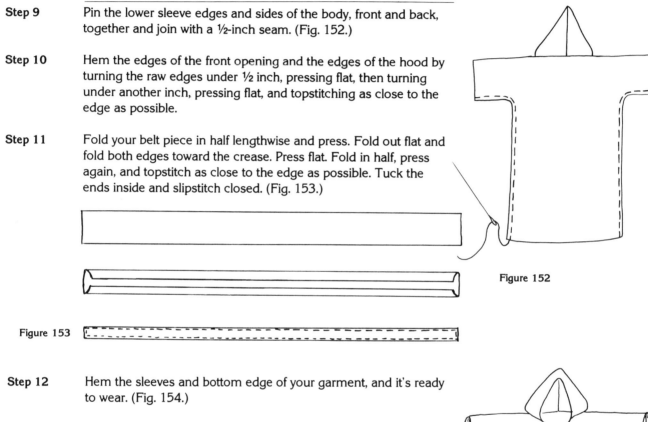

Figure 152

Figure 153

Step 12   Hem the sleeves and bottom edge of your garment, and it's ready to wear. (Fig. 154.)

Optional   If you would like to add pockets, do so now.

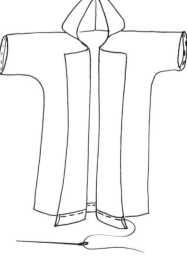

Figure 154

T-Shirt Halter Top

Materials	A large size, strap-style cotton undershirt. Optional: fabric dye, paint, and trim.

These halter tops are a snap to make. They're cool and comfortable and mold to the beautiful contours of a pregnant body. We have used men's summer T-shirts, and since the material is so thin, we use fabric paint to create a concealing design to avert the scandal of peek-a-boo nipples.

Lately, we've discovered T-shirts in heavier cotton that are available in women's sizes and can be ordered through Sears and Roebuck or J. C. Penney. They can be found in the women's underwear section of the catalog. Order the large size or, for a looser fit, order extra large. The cotton lends itself well to batiking or tie-dyeing. Before you dye or decorate, be sure to wash the shirt to remove the sizing.

We've decorated these shirts with Versatex, a fabric paint that can be purchased in art supply stores. The bright colors stay soft and don't fade or run.

You can also decorate these T-shirts with simple bias tape edgings, or fancier lace trims will also snazz up your T-shirt. Appliqués, either the sew-on or iron-on kind, can be used to add a scenic decoration, your initials, or, if you've got one, a message to the world.

Step 1   Cut the straps on the back of the T-shirt. On some T-shirts, the back portion is built up to meet the strap. If this is the case, you will need to cut this portion and turn the raw edge under. (Fig. 156.)

Step 2   If you're a perfectionist, you can finish the strap by tucking the raw edges under and slipstitching them closed. (Fig. 157.)

Step 3   Decorate with dye, fabric paint, batik, embroidery, or trim. (Fig. 158.)

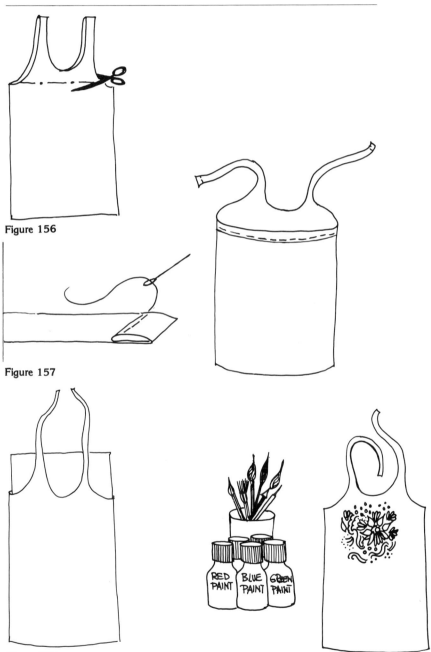

Figure 156

Figure 157

Figure 158

Sun Top

101

Figure 160

Materials	1 yard of 45- or 54-inch-wide polyester. 1½ yards of waistband elastic.

We made this one with warm climates and summertime pregnancies in mind. However, in colder climates, you could wear it over your favorite turtleneck, which is probably creeping over the top of your belly about now.

The length of your finished top will, of course, depend on how wide a fabric you choose. A 45-inch width will give you a 42-inch-long garment, and 54-inch width will give you a 51-inch-long top. Although we've never tried it, it did occur to us that this top could be a dress by simply making it longer. In a nice, soft, clingy fabric like Qiana, it might be quite attractive and certainly comfortable. If you decide to venture out into the unknown, send us a snapshot of the final results.

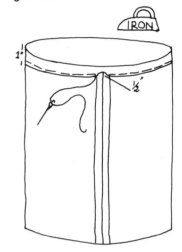

Figure 161

Step 1 Fold the material in half lengthwise and make a ½-inch seam on the selvage edges. (Fig. 160.)

Step 2 To form the casing for your elastic, fold the top edge under 1 inch and iron flat. You won't need to turn the edges under twice for this casing since you are working with polyester, which doesn't unravel. Stitch all around the top edge ¼ inch from the raw edge leaving a ½-inch opening at the side seam for putting in the elastic. (Fig. 161.)

Step 3 Thread the elastic through the casing with a safety pin. Slip the garment on, adjust the elastic, pin it in place, and cut. Sew the ends of the elastic together and slipstitch the opening closed. (Fig. 162.)

Step 4 Determine the length you want for your top and mark the hem. Sew the hem, and your garment is ready to wear.

Figure 162

Adjustable Swimsuit

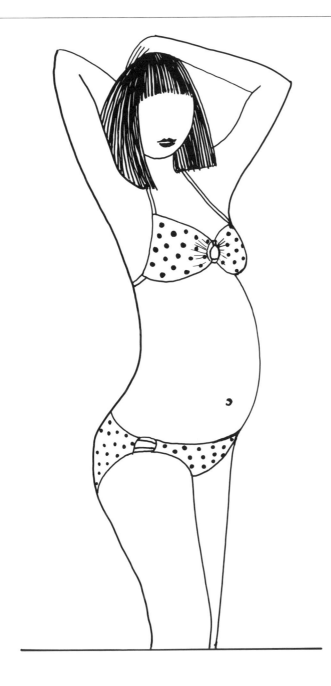

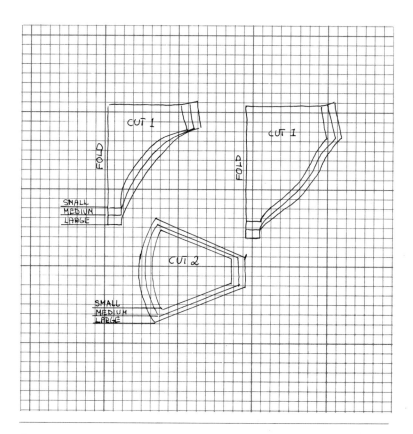

Figure 164

Materials

¾ yard of 45-inch-wide chlorine-resistant bathing suit material.
3 yards of ⅜-inch elastic. (Fig. 163.)

This bathing suit will grow along with you and the baby. The ties on the top and on the sides will allow for lots of adjusting. After the baby comes and you're the figure of your former self, all you have to do is tighten the ties, and it's a perfect fit once again.

The chemicals used in most pools are murder on fabric. The interaction of chlorine and sunlight is guaranteed to bleach out those pretty colors, so be sure to ask for chlorine-resistant swimsuit material when you're shopping for fabric. Ideally, this fabric should be stitched on a zigzag machine, but don't fret if you don't have one. Just be sure to use polyester thread and a needle designed for knits.

Step 1

Select the appropriate size and, using the guide given here, make and mark your own pattern. (Fig. 164.)

Step 2

Fold your fabric in half lengthwise. Pin your pattern pieces on the fabric and cut. (Fig. 165.)

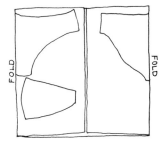

Figure 165

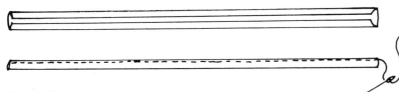

Figure 166

Step 3	To make the ties, fold each of your three tie pieces in half lengthwise, right sides facing. Pin together and make a seam ½ inch from the edge. Trim the seam and turn the ties right side out. Tuck the raw edges inside and slipstitch closed. Iron flat. (Fig. 166.)

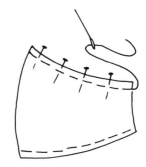

Figure 167

Step 4 Take the two trapezoid-shaped pieces that will form the top of your suit and turn the top and bottom edges under ½ inch to form the casing for the elastic. Pin and stitch. (Fig. 167.)

Step 5 Next, cut four lengths of elastic. If you are making a small suit, each piece will be 6½ inches long; for a medium, each will be 7½ inches long; for a large, each will be 8 inches long. Then, thread the elastic through the top and bottom casings and secure with a few stitches on the inside and outside edges. (Fig. 168.)

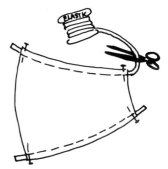

Figure 168

Step 6 Turn the inside edges and the outside curved edges under ¾ inch to form the casings for your ties. Pin and stitch. (Fig. 169.)

Step 7 Take one of your ties and thread it from the bottom to the top of one side and the top to the bottom of the other side. This will be tied behind your back. Then, take another tie and thread it from the bottom of the inside edge to the top on one side and from the top to the bottom on the other side, and tie. This will allow you to adjust the suit as you grow. (Fig. 170.)

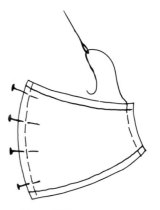

Figure 169

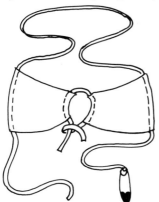

Figure 170

Step 8   Now, for the bottom half of your suit. Place the front and back pieces together, right sides facing and make a ½-inch seam along the crotch line. Press the seam open. Topstitch on each side of the seam so it won't be uncomfortable when you're wearing the suit. (Fig. 171.)

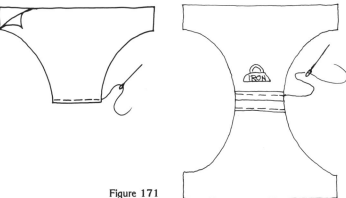

Figure 171

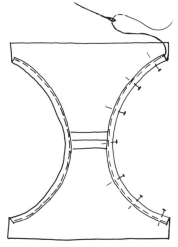

Figure 172

Step 9   To form the leg casing, fold the leg edges under ½ inch and pin in place. Since you are working on a curve, you should probably baste the edge before you do the final stitching. Topstitch as close to the edge as possible. (Fig. 172.)

Step 10   Next, cut two lengths of elastic, one for each leg. For a small suit you will need 26½-inch-long pieces; for a medium, 28-inch-long; and for a large, 30-inch-long. Use a safety pin to thread the elastic through the casing and secure with a few stitches at either end. (Fig. 173.)

Step 11   To form the casing for the waist, turn the waist edge under ½ inch, front and back. Pin in place and topstitch as close to the edge as possible. (Fig. 174.)

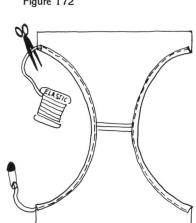

Figure 173

Step 12   Cut two lengths of elastic for the waist. If you are making a small suit, cut a piece 13½ inches long for the front and one 14 inches long for the back; for a medium, cut the front piece 14 inches long and the back piece 15 inches long; for a large, cut the front piece 15 inches long and the back piece 16 inches long. Using a safety

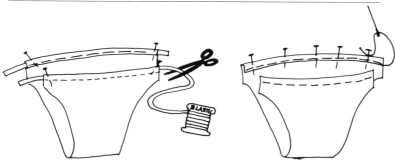

Figure 174   Figure 175

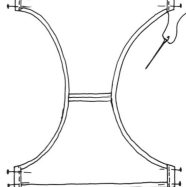

pin, thread the elastic through the casing and secure on all ends with a few stitches. (Fig. 175.)

Step 13   To make the tie casings, turn the side edges under ¾ inch on either side of the front and back pieces. Topstitch as close to the edge as possible. (Fig. 176.)

Step 14   Thread a tie from top to bottom and bottom to top on each side. Try the garment on, tying looser or tighter to adjust the size. (Fig. 177.)

Figure 176

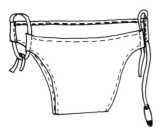

Figure 177

Recycled

Square Scarf Halter Top

111

Materials	One or two large square scarfs, approximately 34 x 34 inches. Optional: one or two small scarfs, approximately 24 x 24 inches.

You needn't sew a single stitch. With just a twist here and a knot there, you can create a whole wardrobe of halter tops. If you don't already have a collection of scarfs, you can make your own by simply turning the edges of a fabric remnant under and hemming or piecing together bits of leftover scraps to make a patchwork scarf.

You'll find that cotton scarfs work better than the silkier ones, which tend to slip. The scarfs will stay in place even better if you dampen them slightly before tying them.

Simple triangle To make the version shown here, simply fold your scarf in half diagonally to form a triangle and tie in the back. (Fig. 179.)

Bandeau For this version, fold the scarf on the diagonal to form a triangle again. Next, fold the tip of the triangle to meet the base. Knot in the front or the back. (Fig. 180.)

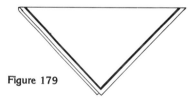

Figure 179

Figure 180

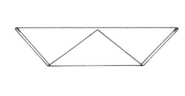

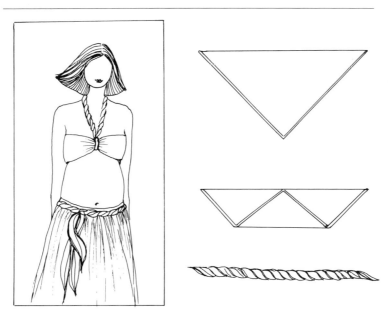

Figure 181

Halter bra   For this one you'll need two scarfs. Fold one of your scarfs in half on the diagonal to form a triangle. Then, fold the tip of the triangle to its base. Wrap the folded scarf around your bosom and tie in the front or back. Then, take the second scarf and fold it the same way. Twist or roll it, pull it through the center, and tie it around your neck. (Fig. 181.)

Optional   Add a complimentary headwrap by taking a small square scarf, folding it into a triangle, and tying it low over the eyebrows, letting the tail hang free. Or, for a fancier version, tuck the tail under the knot to hide it. Then, take a second small scarf, fold it into a triangle, roll into a tube, and twist. Center over your forehead, tie in the back, and tuck the ends under the front. (Fig. 182.)

Figure 182

Rectangular Scarf Halter Wrap

Materials	Long rectangular scarf, about 10 inches wide and 6 feet long.
Optional	Tablecloth-sized scarf, approximately 42 x 42 inches. (Fig. 183.)

If you don't have a scarf long enough for these halter wraps, try sewing a couple of scarfs together. Or, if you have a large scrap of material, try cutting a diagonal strip out of the center as shown. Then, take each of the smaller pieces and cut them to form equilateral triangles. Turn the raw edges under, hem, and you've got three scarfs from one piece of material.

Choker style Wrap the scarf around your neck, choker style. Cross in the back or front and tie as shown. (Fig. 184.)

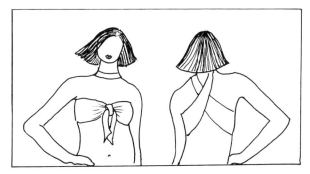

Figure 184

Crisscross wrap Take the scarf and loop it around your neck. Cross in the front and tie in the back. (Fig. 185.)

Underarm wrap Loop the scarf around your neck and under your arms. Cross it in the back and bring it around the front to tie. (Fig. 186.)

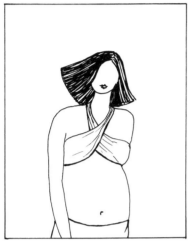

Figure 185

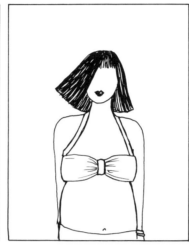

Figure 186

Optional   To make a headwrap, take your tablecloth-sized scarf, fold it into a triangle, and center low on forehead. Knot twice in the back, once under the tail and once again over it. Twist each end slightly and bring them around to the front. Cross the ends over each other, return to the back, and knot under the tail. (Fig. 187.)

Figure 187

Four-Scarf Skirt

118

Materials	Four large square scarfs. ½-inch waistband elastic, the length equal to that of your waist measurement plus 10 inches.

The hem of this skirt hangs with a graceful unevenness. We made ours from 34-inch-square scarfs with patterns blended well together. If you are short, you may want to use smaller scarfs. You can gauge the final length of your skirt at its shortest points by subtracting the diameter of your waistband circle (see Step 4) plus 1 inch for the waistband casing from the length of your scarf. For example, we used a 7-inch diameter for our waist circle, and added 1 inch for the casing, which equals 8 inches. If you subtract 8 inches from 34 inches (the length of the scarf), you get 26 inches, which, sure enough, was the exact length of our finished skirt at its shortest point. Spend a few moments calculating these measurements so you don't use scarfs that will produce a skirt that is either too short or too long. Of course, if your skirt does turn out to be too short, you can always add an extra tier of scarfs or wear the skirt above your bustline as a sleeveless top.

Step 1 Take two of your scarfs and lay them on top of each other as shown, with right sides facing each other. Sew them together with a ½-inch seam. Open the seams and press. Do the same with the other two scarfs. Then, join all four scarfs together to form one large square of scarfs. (Fig. 189.)

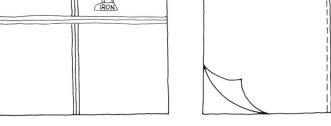
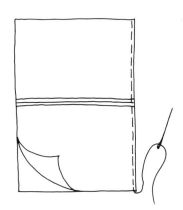

Figure 189

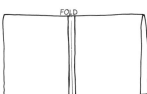

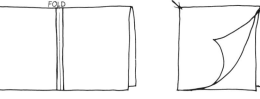

Figure 190

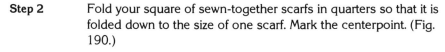

Figure 191

Step 2 Fold your square of sewn-together scarfs in quarters so that it is folded down to the size of one scarf. Mark the centerpoint. (Fig. 190.)

Step 3 Now you will want to cut the circle that will become the waist of your skirt. If your pre-pregnancy size was petite, use a 6-inch diameter; if it was small, a 7-inch diameter; medium, an 8-inch diameter; and large, a 9-inch diameter. Cut a piece of string the proper length and tack one end to the centerpoint. Tie a piece of marking chalk or a fabric pencil to the other end and draw a quarter circle or arc. Cut along the line you have drawn. (Fig. 191.)

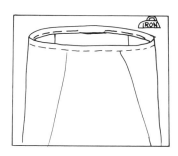

Figure 192

Step 4 Open up your scarfs. If you have a zigzag stitch on your machine, you can turn the raw edges of your waist circle under ¾ inch, press, and topstitch to form the casing. Or, you can sew a length of stretch lace or seam tape to the raw edges, turn under for a ¾-inch casing, press flat, and topstitch along the bottom edge. Don't forget to leave a ½-inch opening along a seam so that you can insert your elastic. (Fig. 192.)

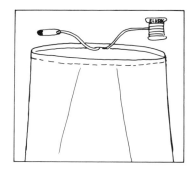

Figure 193

Step 5 Attach a safety pin to the elastic and thread it through the casing. Put the skirt on and adjust the gathers and elastic. Pin the ends of the elastic in place. Remove the garment and cut the end of the elastic, leaving an excess of 10 inches. Tuck the excess inside the casing. Secure the elastic with several stitches, and slipstitch the opening closed. (Fig. 193.)

Step 6 Slip your finished skirt on, grab a couple of scarfs, wrap yourself a halter top, and you're all ready to go.

Drawstring Scarf Skirt

Materials   A collection of scarfs of equal length that have a combined width equal to approximately 2 yards. 1 ½ yards of decorative cord or braid for drawstring.

Once upon a time, not so long ago, the dresser scarf was an absolute must. Every bureau, table, and dresser was draped with these decorative, embroidered scarfs that also served to protect the natural wood of the furniture. Nowadays, in our world of Formica, plastic-coated wood surfaces, and spray-on acrylic waxes, the dresser scarf is no longer a necessity. We've managed to put our old dresser scarfs to good use in this skirt. It may take a bit of patching together, sewing shorter, nightstand scarfs together to equal the length of a dresser scarf, but the effort is well worth it. If you have to patch smaller scarfs, you will want to even up the raw edges at the top of your skirt so you can keep those delicate embroidered hems intact at the lower edge of your skirt.

This skirt also works well when made from those long rectangular Indian print cotton scarfs that were so popular a couple of years back. No matter what kind of scarfs you use, you will have to make sure that they are the same length. If you have scarfs of unequal length, you can cut them down so they are all of equal length. Here again, remember that you will want the raw edges to be folded down for the drawstring casing, leaving the prehemmed edges for the bottom of your skirt.

Step 1   Lay two of your scarfs on top of one another, right sides facing. Pin and join together with a ½-inch seam. Repeat this process until you have joined together enough scarfs to form a 2-yard-wide patchwork of scarfs. (Fig. 195.)

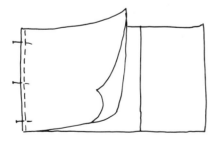

Figure 195

Step 2   Fold your joined-together scarfs in half crosswise, right sides facing. Pin and make a ½-inch seam long the edge as shown here. Press the seam open. (Fig. 196.)

Step 3   Turn the top edge under ½ inch and press flat. Turn it under again, 1 inch this time, and press. Topstitch as close to the edge as possible, leaving a ½-inch opening in the front, opposite your seam, for the drawstring. Reinforce this opening by backstitching a couple of times on either side of it. (Fig. 197.)

Step 4   Thread your cord or braid through the drawstring casing with a safety pin. Knot the ends of the drawstring to prevent it from working back through the casing in the wash. Since your scarfs are already hemmed, you needn't bother with that. Just slip your skirt on and show it off. (Fig. 198.)

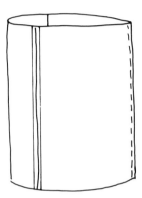

Figure 196

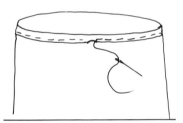

Figure 197

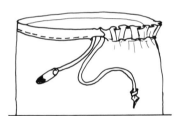

Figure 198

Eight-Scarf Dress

Materials	Eight large square scarfs.

As the name implies, this lovely, flowing dress can be made from eight large square scarfs. If you keep your eyes open, you can find real silk scarfs at thrift shops, rummage sales, and so on, and make yourself a genuine silk dress for just a few dollars!

This garment can be worn alone or with pants. It can also be worn over a leotard. If you buy a leotard that is one or two sizes larger than your normal size, you'll be able to wear it during most of your pregnancy. It not only feels comfortable and offers extra support, but looks great under this dress.

Step 1   Lay out scarfs A and B and lay scarf C in the middle so that the edges of scarf C overlap the edges of A and B about ¼ inch on either side. Pin in place and topstitch the scarfs together. (Fig. 200.)

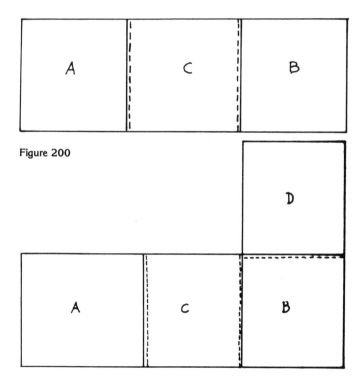

Figure 200

Figure 201

Step 2　Lay scarf D next to scarf B with the edges overlapping about ¼ inch. Pin and topstitch D to B. (Fig. 201.)

Step 3　Bring the edge of scarf D to the edge of scarf A as indicated. Overlap ¼ inch, pin, and topstitch scarfs A and D together to form the bodice of your dress. (Fig. 202.)

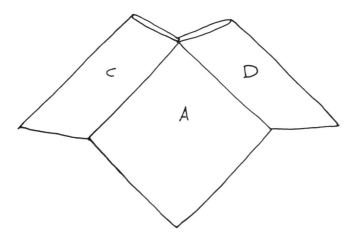

Figure 202

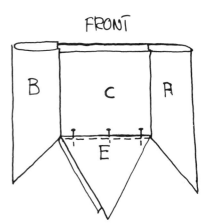

Step 4　Take scarf E, which will form one side of your dress, and fold on the diagonal so that the diagonal fold is the same length as the bottom edge of scarf C. Overlap the edges ¼ inch and stitch in place. Repeat the same process with scarf F, and stitch it to scarf D. (Fig. 203.)

Step 5　Take your last two scarfs, G and H, and fold them in half lengthwise. These will form the sleeves of your dress and the folded edge will become the top edge of the sleeve. (Fig. 204.)

Figure 204

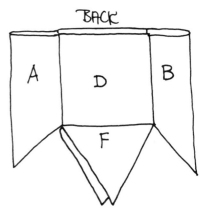

Figure 203

Step 6   Find the centerfront (the tip of scarf A) and the centerback (the tip of scarf B) of your garment. Mark points 3 inches from the center-points, front and back. Starting at these points, pin scarfs G and H to scarfs C and D so that the edges overlap about ¼ inch. (Fig. 205.)

Step 7   Try your dress on, being careful not to stick yourself with the pins. Check to see that the neckline is comfortable for you. Check the armholes. Pinning the sleeves under the arms may be uncomfortable. If so, take out a few pins and don't sew all the way under the arms. After you have adjusted and removed your garment, top-stitch scarfs G and H, and that's all there is to it. (Fig. 206.)

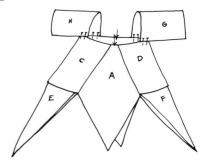

Figure 205

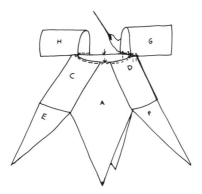

Figure 206

Scarf Shawl

Materials A rectangular scarf, at least 42 x 15 inches. 2 yards of narrow satin ribbon. Optional: assorted sequins and stars, embroidery thread, or fabric paint.

This scarf shawl won't keep you too warm, but it will accent any outfit. If you've made a scarf dress or one of the scarf skirts out of chiffon, silk, or rayon scarfs, this shawl can add a romantic look to your outfit. If the scarfs you've used for your dress or skirt are solid, soft pastels, you might try painting with fabric paint or sewing lines of sequins and stars to your shawl. If you've made a dresser-scarf skirt, look for an extra long one to finish your outfit with a dresser-scarf shawl. Contrasting colors in the shawl and the scarf skirts also work well. Likewise, any scarf with a border print will make a great shawl.

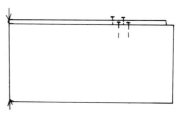

Figure 208

Step 1 Hold the scarf around you so that it falls the way you would like to wear it. Mark the places where you're holding it with pins. (Fig. 208.)

Step 2 Cut your ribbon into four pieces, each 18 inches long. Turn the ends of the ribbon under and sew to the scarf in the places you have marked with pins. (Fig. 209.)

Step 3 If desired, you can embroider or paint your shawl. Wet silk and fabric paint or acrylics are a phenomenal experience, or sew wiggly lines of sequins and stars radiating out from the ribbon ties. Use an embroidery hoop to make it easier to sew on the sequins or to paint. (Fig. 210.)

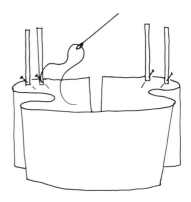

Figure 209

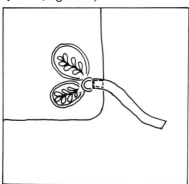

Figure 210

Scarf Bikini

Materials	Four 22 x 22-inch cotton scarfs.

This one lets you get a little sunshine on your belly. Your investment is minimal, just four scarfs and a few stitches, and you've got a bikini. Use cotton scarfs though; silky scarves tend to slip, which could get complicated unless you're sunning at a nude beach. Dampening the scarfs before tying them on will help you keep your suit, as will twisting the ends to take up any slack before tying them.

Step 1	To make the top, fold two of the scarfs in thirds and tie them together. Center the knot between your breasts and tie the other ends behind your neck. (Fig. 212.)

Figure 212

Step 2	To make the bottom, fold your other two scarfs into triangles. Place the tips of the triangle together so that they overlap. (Fig. 213.)
Step 3	Sew the tips together as shown to form the crotch. Twist and tie firmly at the hips, and you're ready to stretch out poolside or at the beach. (Fig. 214.)

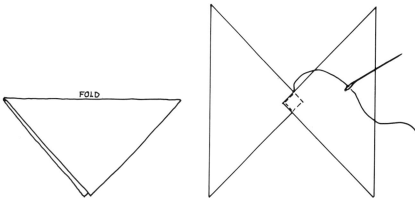

FOLD

Figure 213   Figure 214

Pillowcase Skirt

Materials	Two pillowcases. ¾-inch waistband elastic, length equal to your waist plus 10 inches. Optional: rickrack or other decorative trim.

The length of your finished skirt will depend on whether you use standard-size pillowcases, which will give you a short skirt; queen-size pillowcases, which will give you a midi-length; or king-size cases, which will give you a long skirt. Pillowcases with borders or embroidered edges work best. You could also trim a plain case with rows of rickrack or other trim. Try layering skirts one on top of the other for a peasant effect. If you decide to layer your skirts, make sure one of them is white and ruffly. Top your skirt off with a T-shirt halter top and a pillowcase shawl or pull it up over your bust and wear it as a sundress or blouse.

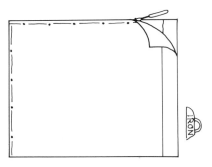

Step 1   Open the top and side seams of your pillowcases and iron them flat. (Fig. 216.)

Figure 216

Step 2   Determine what length you want your finished skirt to be and add 1½ inches to this measurement to allow for the waistband casing. Measure this length from the bottom, prehemmed edge of your pillowcases. Mark carefully so that you have a straight edge on the top of your pillowcases, and cut off any excess fabric. (Fig. 217.)

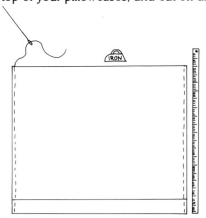

Figure 217

Step 3   Lay your pillowcases together, right sides facing, and pin the side seams together, starting from the bottom so your hems will be even. Stitch a ½-inch seam and iron the seams open. (Fig. 218.)

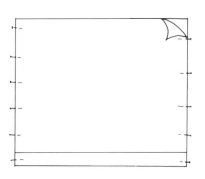

Figure 218

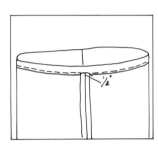

Figure 219

Figure 220

Step 4   To make the casing for the waistband, fold the top edge under
½ inch and iron flat. Then, fold under another inch and press
again. Topstitch as close as possible to the bottom edge, leaving a
2-inch opening for threading the elastic. (Fig. 219.)

Step 5   Thread your elastic through the casing. Then, slip the skirt on and
adjust for a proper fit. Pin the elastic in place. Remove the skirt and
sew the elastic together, leaving an extra 10 inches of elastic to
allow for expansion of the waistline. Tuck the excess elastic into the
casing. Slipstitch the opening closed. (Fig. 220.)

Optional   If you plan to add trim, do so now.

Pillowcase Shawl

Materials   One pillowcase, standard, king, or queen size. Optional: one or more types of trim.

This shawl will keep your shoulders warm on a cool summer night and looks great with a pillowcase skirt. The type of trim you select might be coordinated with the trim on your skirt. If, for instance, you trimmed the hem of your skirt with three rows of increasingly thinner rickrack, you might want to trim your shawl in the same way. If you are using a standard-size pillowcase, you will need to add 1 ¾ yards of trim — white, ruffled eyelet, for example — to make the shawl a bit larger. If you are making a shawl from a queen-size pillowcase and you want to add trim, you will need 2 yards; for a king size, 2 ¼ yards.

If you have chosen a patterned pillowcase for your skirt, you might want to make the shawl from a pillowcase with the same pattern, but in a different color. If you've layered one skirt over another, try making the shawl out of the same color and pattern pillowcase as the bottom layer of your skirt.

Step 1   Open the side and top seams of your pillowcase. Iron flat. Cut off the pillowcase hem so that you have a rectangular piece of fabric. (Fig. 222.)

Step 2   From this rectangle, you will cut a square with sides equal to the shortest side of the rectangle. (Fig. 223.)

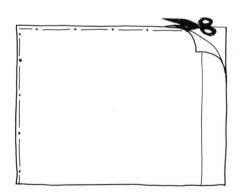   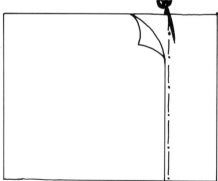

Figure 222   **Figure 223**

Step 3   With the right sides together, fold the square in half to form a triangle. (Fig. 224.)

Step 4   Sew the open edges together with a ½-inch seam, leaving a 4-inch opening on the center of one side. Clip the corners, turn right side out, and slipstitch the opening closed. Iron flat. Topstitch along the sides of the triangle. (Fig. 225.)

Optional   If you use trim, pin it in place and stitch down. (Fig. 226.)

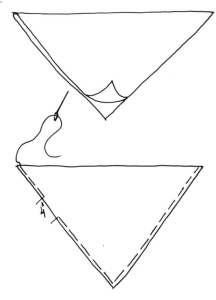

Figure 224

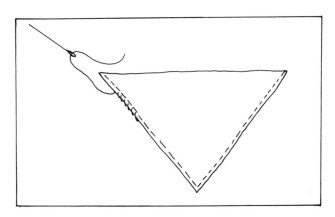

Figure 225

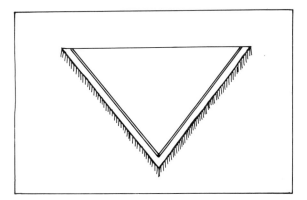

Figure 226

Sheet Kimono

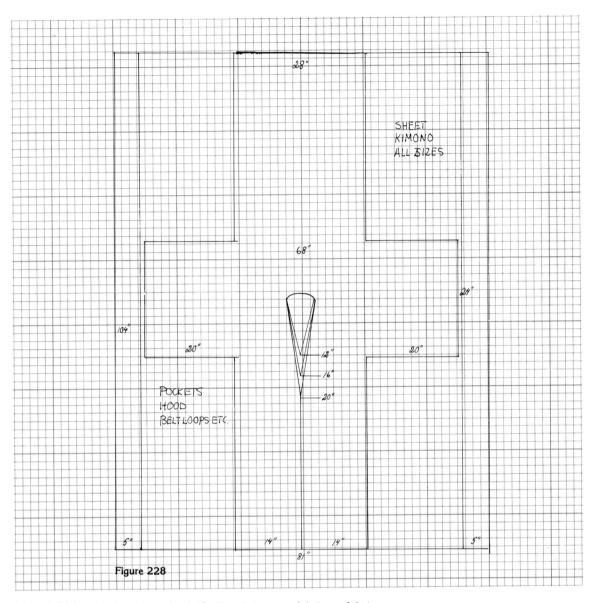

Figure 228

Materials	81 by 104-inch flat double sheet. Optional: iron-on fabric or fabric paint.

Since you've already used up all your pillowcases making the skirts and shawls, you might as well make use of those leftover sheets. We made our first kimono from a plain white sheet and decorated it with Oriental-style designs cut from iron-on fabric. The next one was made from a pretty floral pattern. Then, we got classy and made one from the sexy black silk satin topsheet we'd gotten as a wedding present (having long since worn out the bottom sheet getting pregnant).

Step 1	Enlarge and reproduce the pattern given here. (Or, if you're feeling particularly brave or full of progesterone, you might be able to mark and cut your sheet without making a pattern by using chalk or a fabric-marking pen.) (Fig. 228.)

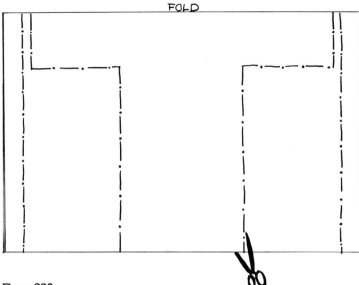

FOLD

Figure 229

Step 2   Fold your sheet in half crosswise. Pin your pattern in place. Mark the fabric, and cut the main pieces from the fabric. (Fig. 229.)

Step 3   Open your kimono out so that it lies flat and cut the neck and front openings. (Fig. 230.)

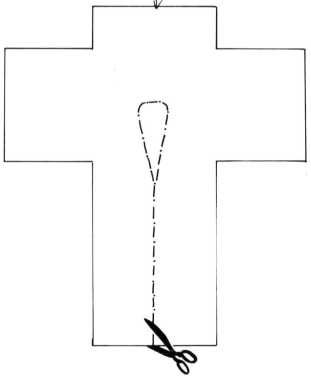

Figure 230

Step 4   Take one of the long strips you have cut and fold it in half crosswise. Mark the centerpoint. This will become the front band of your
kimono. Match the centerpoint of the band to the center back of
the neck. Pin the band to the kimono body all around the neck and
front edges. Baste first, then join the pieces together with a ½-inch
seam. (Fig. 231.)

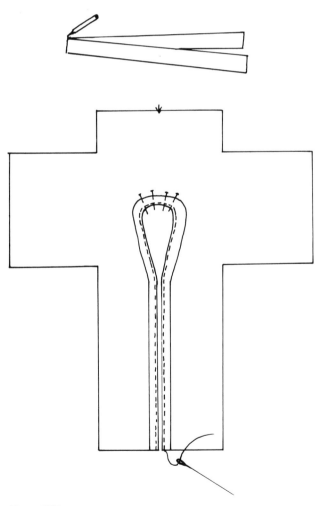

Figure 231

Step 5   Press the seam toward the band. Turn the raw edge of the band under ½ inch and press flat. Then fold the band in half and press it again. (Fig. 232.)

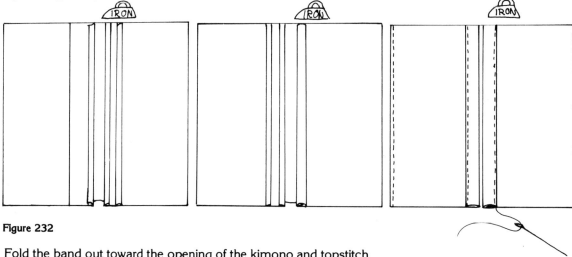

Figure 232

Step 6   Fold the band out toward the opening of the kimono and topstitch as close to the edge as possible. (Fig. 233.)

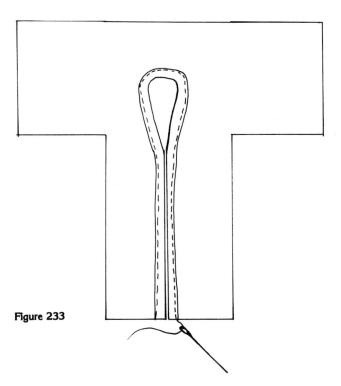

Figure 233

Step 7   Pin the sleeve and side seams together and join them with a
½-inch seam. Slash the underarm seams and iron all seams open.
(Fig. 234.)

Step 8   Turn the lower edges of your garment and sleeves under and hem.
It may be necessary to cut the sheet hem from the kimono to avoid
a too bulky hem. (Fig. 235.)

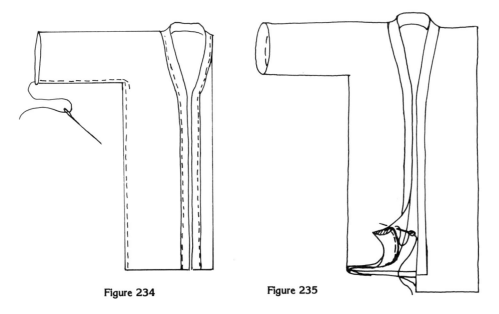

Figure 234   Figure 235

Step 9   Take your remaining long strip of material, fold the raw edges
under ½ inch on either side, and press flat. Fold the band in half
lengthwise, press, and topstitch along the entire length. Cut your
belt to the desired length. Tuck the ends in and slipstitch closed.
(Fig. 236.)

Figure 236

Optional Cut Oriental-type designs from a contrasting color of iron-on fabric, sprinkle them over the shoulders and bodice, and iron in place. If you prefer, paint Oriental characters on your fabric. Trimming the edges of your sleeves and band will also give your garment that finishing touch. (Fig. 237.)

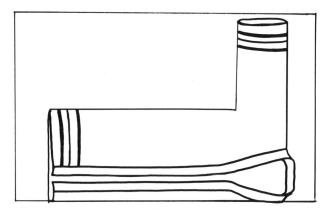

Figure 237

Bath Towel Kimono

Materials	Three large bath towels. Optional: trim.

This kimono can be put together inside of an hour and can be worn throughout your pregnancy and afterward as well. We used three of those large, fluffy bath towels, 30 by 46 inches each, that have a looped side and a furry side. If you use towels with differently textured sides, you will need to pay attention to right and wrong sides when assembling this garment or you could end up with a kimono that has a furry top and a looped bottom. Although, come to think of it, that might be okay, too.

The kimono can be decorated with rickrack, ribbon, or any desired trim. Plan your trim and measure the towels to figure how much trim to buy.

Step 1 Fold one towel in half lengthwise, right side (if there is one) facing you. Mark the center of the folded edge and the center of the bottom edges. In the middle of the folded edge, cut an 8-inch slit (A-B). This will become the neck opening, so slip it over your head to make sure it fits easily. If necessary, make the opening slightly larger, until it fits comfortably. Now, finish the neck by turning the raw edges under and topstitching or by using seam tape. If you plan to add trim to the top of your garment, pin in place and topstitch now. (Fig. 239.)

Figure 239

Step 2 Next, you will need to measure the length of your skirt. Put the top piece on, align the centerpoints, and measure the distance to the floor. Add ½ inch for the seam. Then, cut your two remaining towels to the desired length. Mark the centerpoint on each of the raw edges. (Fig. 240.)

Step 3 If you plan to add trim to the lower portions of your garment, pin and topstitch in place. Then, gather each of the two remaining towels along the edges you have just cut. Gathering along this edge rather than the uncut edge will save you from having to hem the finished garment. Pin the long edges of the towels together, making sure that the right sides are facing each other. (Fig. 241.)

Step 4 Now, slip your pinned garment on to check the fit, adjusting the gathers as necessary, and remembering that the gathers must be loose enough to allow you to pull it on over your head. Make sure

Figure 240

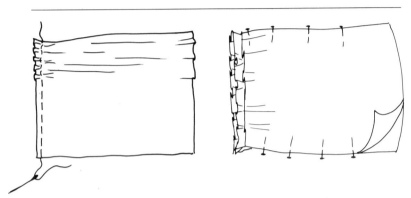

Figure 241

the gathers are distributed evenly on both sides, using the center-points as a guide. Then, remove the garment and stitch the seams, leaving a slit at the bottom of each side to allow for freedom of movement. The length of the slit should be equal to the number of inches between your knee and the floor. (Fig. 242.)

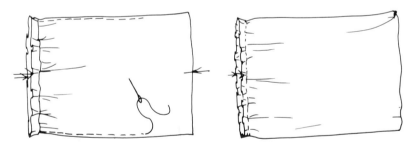

Figure 242   **Figure 243**

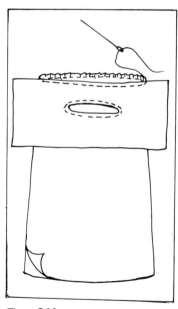

Figure 244

Step 5   Now, turn the bottom piece that you've been working on right-side out so the right sides of the towels are facing you. Make sure the centerpoints of each of the gathered edges are aligned. (Fig. 243.)

Step 6   Spread your top piece out, wrong side facing you and lay it on top of the gathered piece, edges even, and centers matching. Pin the bottom edge of your top piece to one of the gathered edges and join with a ½-inch seam. (Fig. 244.)

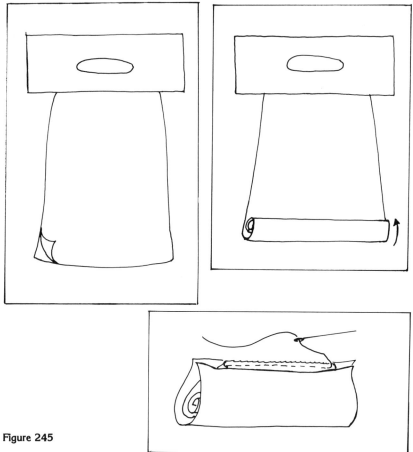

Figure 245

Step 7   Fold the top piece out. Roll the bottom piece up onto the top piece until the unseamed gathered edge that was underneath is facing you. Pin the centerpoint of the unseamed gathered edge to the centerpoint of the bottom of the top piece. (Don't give up if the instructions seem unclear at this point. It's a bit awkward to explain, but once you are actually doing it, everything will become quite clear. Trust us!) Now, pin the edges together and join with a ½-inch seam. (Fig. 245.)

Step 8   Sew the sleeve seams, leaving the last two inches open for freedom of movement. Turn the garment right-side out. Pat yourself on the head, and admire yourself in front of the mirror. (Fig. 246.)

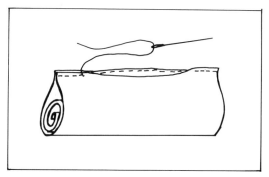

Figure 246

Beach Wrap

Materials   Two large towels, 26 x 50 inches. 1 yard of Velcro stripping.
1¼ yards of ½-inch elastic.

Now that we've emptied your linen closet of sheets, pillowcases, blankets, and towels, you'd think we'd be satisfied, but don't close the door yet. You'll need two more large-size bath or beach towels for this simple wrap. We used 26 x 50-inch towels, but dimensions are not critical as long as you have sufficient width. Here again, you'll want to pay attention to the looped and furry sides of your towels, and you might want to match patterns when laying out your towels.

We used Velcro strips to close the front of our wrap. (Velcro consists of one strip of nylon tape covered with tiny hooks and another strip of pile fabric with tiny loops. When the two are pressed together, they stick until pulled apart. Velcro is available at any good fabric store.)

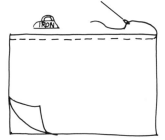

Figure 248

Step 1   Lay your towels together, right sides facing, and make a ½-inch seam along one side to form the back of your wrap. Press the seam open. (Fig. 248.)

Step 2   Turn top edge under 1 inch to form the casing for your elastic. Stitch casing along the bottom edge as shown here. We also stitched the casing along the top about ¼ inch from the edge so there would be a nice ruffled edge on the top when we inserted the elastic. (Fig. 249.)

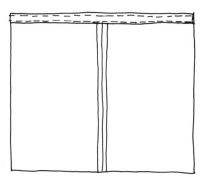

Figure 249

Step 3   Attach a safety pin to your elastic and thread it through the casing. Try it on and adjust gathers. Pin each end of the elastic for a snug fit. Cut the elastic, leaving an extra 3 inches on one end in case you need to make an adjustment as your chest gets larger. Tuck the excess elastic neatly in one end of the casing. Sew the ends of elastic firmly in place. (Fig. 250.)

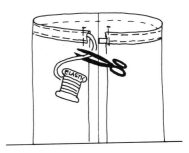

Figure 250

Step 4   To attach the Velcro, first take the pile/loop strip and, starting at the top edge, pin it to the edge of the under piece of your wrap. Then, stitch over the strip by machine or by hand several times to hold it in place. Pin the hook strip to the inside of the front edge of the overlapping front piece of the wrap. Slipstitch in place by hand or topstitch by machine through all layers of fabric for a decorative design detail. (Fig. 251.)

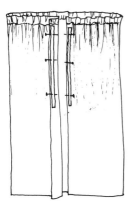

Figure 251

Blanket Poncho

Materials   A blanket. Heavy duty thread. Optional: 4–10 yards of narrow-band blanket binding for finishing the edges.

We used our favorite fuzzy blanket for this poncho. It measured 62 x 83 inches, but the garment is loose-fitting so the dimensions are not critical. If you have a zigzag stitch on your machine, you can finish the raw edges of your poncho with a simple zigzag stitch. If not, use narrow-band blanket binding, which is available in most fabric stores. You will need about 4 yards to trim the raw edges on a poncho made from a 62 x 83-inch blanket; however, you may want to bind all the edges, perhaps in a contrasting color, to give your garment a more finished look. In this case, you will need approximately 10 yards of blanket binding to finish the raw edges.

We had a piece of material approximately 11 by 53 inches left over — plenty for a couple of large patch pockets, which came in handy. If you plan to make pockets, you might want extra blanket binding, equal to the length of the sides of the pocket to finish the edges.

Step 1   Cut a strip 11 inches wide from the length of the blanket. Finish the raw edges of the remaining piece of blanket with a zigzag stitch or with blanket binding. (Fig. 253.)

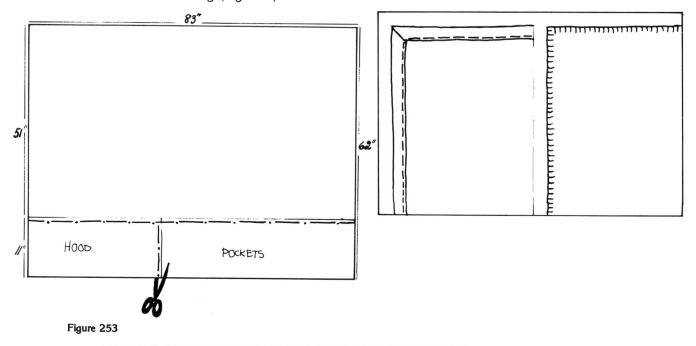

Figure 253

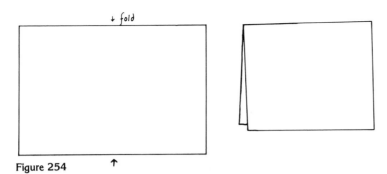

Figure 254

Step 2   Mark the centerpoint, using a yardstick or by folding your large blanket piece in half once and then in half again and marking the point. (Fig. 254.)

Step 3   Reproduce the neck opening pattern given here. Pin the pattern in place, making sure that the pattern and fabric centerpoints are aligned; mark and cut the neck opening. (Fig. 255.)

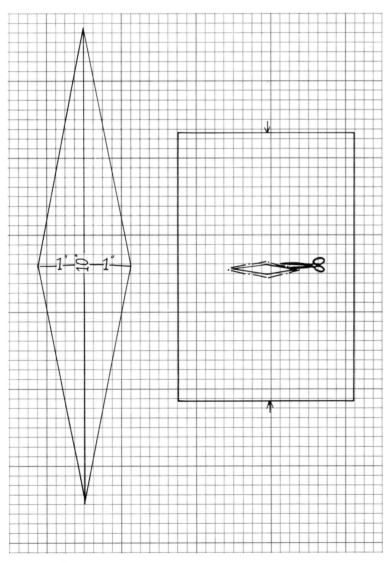

Figure 255

Step 4   Cut a 30-inch piece from the strip that you cut in Step 1 for your hood. Fold the piece in half crosswise, right sides facing. Make a ½-inch seam on the raw edge to form the hood, leaving the selvage edges for the hood front. Finish the lower edges of the hood with zigzag stitching, blanket stitch, or blanket binding. (Fig. 256.)

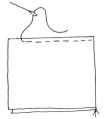

Figure 256

Step 5   Turn the hood right-side out. Pin the bottom edge of the hood around the neck edge of the poncho as shown here, making sure that the hood's back seam is aligned with the back centerpoint of the neck opening. Note that you will be pinning the hood on the outside of the poncho so that the inside of the hood is overlapping the right side of the poncho ½ inch. Stitch in place, leaving the last 2 inches of the hood free on either side to allow for freedom of movement. (Fig. 257.)

Optional   If you are working with a 62 by 83-inch blanket, you will have a leftover strip of material 11 inches wide and 50 inches long. If you want pockets, just cut two identical squares and finish the edges with zigzag stitching or blanket binding. Lay your poncho out, pin the pockets in position, and stitch them in place.

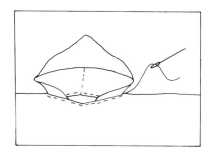

Figure 257

Tablecloth Ensemble

Materials Two tablecloths, one approximately 36 inches in diameter, the other at least 60 inches in diameter. 2½ yards of ribbon.

After the baby comes, you won't have time for formal dinners anyway, so haul out those fancy tablecloths and put them to good use now. If you're not the formal dinner type, you can find an unlimited selection of used tablecloths at most thrift shops. And, if you have some, don't hesitate to use the family heirloom lace cloths. What better time for granny to be with you than in your hour of need?

The style of the outfit you create will depend on the kind of tablecloths you manage to scrounge. Granny's heirloom lace makes for an old-fashioned, romantic look; or, you can create a very elegant outfit with heavy damask linen cloths. For a funky sort of art deco look, use a 1930s-style printed kitchen tablecloth.

For the top of your ensemble, you can use a medium- or large-sized cloth about 36 inches in diameter, although we've made belly-flashing tops out of small tablecloths. Unless you are really petite, you'll need a fairly large cloth for the skirt, probably at least 60 inches in diameter to get the length you want. Measuring the fit is simple enough, just fold the tablecloths in half and hold them up against your body to see if they will be long enough to suit you.

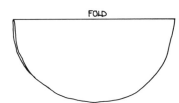

Figure 259

Step 1 The first step is to cut the neck opening in the smaller tablecloth, which will become the blouse. This will be done slightly differently depending on the kind of tablecloth you have.

If you have one of those circular lace cloths with a circle of fabric in the center, cut out the fabric center. For other tablecloths, the following procedure will be more appropriate. Fold your tablecloth in half. Then, fold it in half again. Mark the centerpoint. (Figs. 259 and 260.)

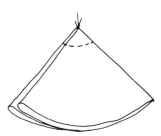

Figure 260

Step 2 Mark two points each 4 inches from the centerpoint on the folded edge. (Fig. 261.)

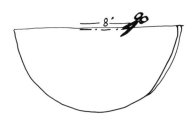

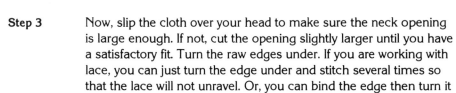

Figure 261

Step 3 Now, slip the cloth over your head to make sure the neck opening is large enough. If not, cut the opening slightly larger until you have a satisfactory fit. Turn the raw edges under. If you are working with lace, you can just turn the edge under and stitch several times so that the lace will not unravel. Or, you can bind the edge then turn it

159

under. Also, if you are working with a lace cloth, you can cut a 1½-yard piece of ribbon and wend it in and out of the top row of lace on your finished neckline and tie a pretty bow. (Fig. 262.)

Step 4 Now you are ready to form the sleeves. Slip your blouse on and adjust the neck so that the blouse hangs properly. Pin the material at a point about 2 to 3 inches below each of your underarms or wherever it feels most comfortable to you. Next, take the top off and make sure that the two pins are evenly placed at the same approximate points on either side of your top. Then, simply tack the arm openings closed.

Some people prefer a more finished sleeve. If you like, you can pin and topstitch a straight line from the point under your arm to the outer edge of the cloth on either side. (Fig. 263.)

Step 5 To make your skirt, you will again need to fold your cloth in quarters and mark the centerpoint. Next, cut a length of string: 5 to 6 inches for a small size, 7 to 8 inches for a medium or large size. Tie a piece of marking chalk or a fabric pencil on one end and push a thumbtack through the other. Tack it to your centerpoint. With the string taut, make an arc by sweeping your chalk across the material. Then, take your scissors and cut along the arc you have just drawn. The circle you have just cut will become the waist of your skirt.

Here again, if you have a large enough lace tablecloth with a sufficiently large fabric center, you can make a waist quite simply just as you would make the lace neckline described in Step 1. (Fig. 264.)

Figure 262

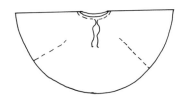

Figure 263

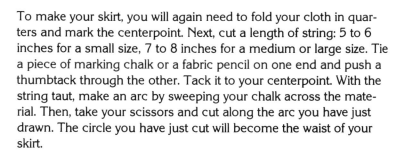

FOLD

(A)   (B)   (C)

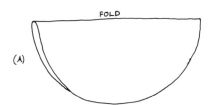

Figure 264

Step 6   If you are working with a lace tablecloth, turn the raw edges under and topstitch several times or bind with seam tape and turn under to prevent the lace from unraveling. Take your remaining yard of ribbon and wend it in and out of the top row of lace to create a drawstring waistband. Otherwise, you will need to make an elastic waist. To make the casing for the elastic, turn the raw edges under ½ inch and press. Turn under another inch, press again, and topstitch all the way around, leaving a 2-inch opening for threading the elastic. Thread the elastic through and try the skirt on. Pin the elastic for a snug fit and cut it, leaving an extra 10 inches to allow for growth. Tuck the excess inside the casing. Secure the elastic with a few stitches and slipstitch the opening closed. (Fig. 265.)

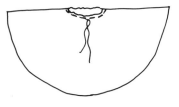 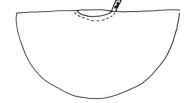

Figure 265

Lace Dress

Materials	A circular lace tablecloth, approximately 68 inches in diameter. ⅔ yard of seam binding.

If you've scoured the junk stores with little luck or if granny only had one lace tablecloth that's survived the generation gap, don't despair. You can make this lace dress, which only requires one large tablecloth. Unless you are really petite, you'll need a tablecloth that's at least 60 inches in diameter. However, if you can't find one that size, use a smaller one and wear your lace dress as a blouse.

Step 1   Fold your tablecloth in half and then in quarters and mark the centerpoint. (Fig. 267.)

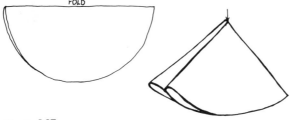

Figure 267

Step 2   Unfold once so that your cloth is only folded in half. To mark your neckline, mark two points on the folded edge, each 5 inches from the centerpoint. Then, mark a point 2 inches below the centerpoint. This point will become the low point of your oval neckline. Mark an arc from the low point of the neckline to the points you have marked on either side of the centerpoint. Cut along this line to form the neckline. (Fig. 268.)

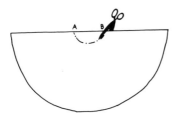

Figure 268

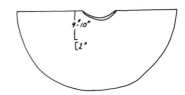

Figure 269

Step 3	Slip the tablecloth on and check the neckline. If you want a lower neckline, you can cut a deeper oval. While you have the garment on, pin it under your arms wherever it feels most comfortable for a sleeve. For most people, this point will be 9 to 10 inches from the folded edge. Remove the tablecloth and check to make sure your underarm pins are equidistant from the folded and outer edges of your tablecloth. Mark two points, each 1 inch lower than the underarm points you have pinned, to allow for seams. (Fig. 269.)

Step 4	Next, you will want to cut the sleeves. Use a yardstick to draw a line from the underarm points to the outer edges of your tablecloth. If you want a straight sleeve, draw a straight line from the underarm point to the outer edge of the tablecloth parallel with the folded edge on either side. If you'd like a fuller sleeve, make your lines fall farther down along the tablecloth edges. Remember that the larger the sleeve, the easier it will be to put the garment on. (Fig. 270.)

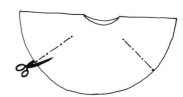

Figure 270

Step 5	Cut along the lines you have drawn. Make a ½-inch seam on the raw edges to form sleeves. Since you are working with lace, you should first bind the edge with seam binding or stitch your seams several times so your lace won't unravel. (Fig. 271.)

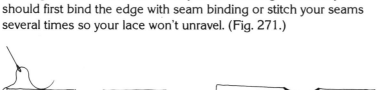

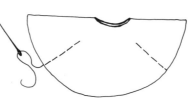

Figure 271

Step 6	Finish your neck by turning under ½ inch and topstitching several times or by binding the raw edges with seam binding. Since the edges of the tablecloth are already finished, you won't have to make a hem; your garment is ready to wear. (Fig. 272.)

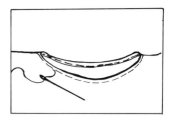

Figure 272

Adding a Maternity Panel

Materials	Your favorite pair of pants or jeans. A premade elasticized maternity panel.

You can easily revamp your favorite pants or jeans so that you can wear them throughout your pregnancy by adding a maternity panel, which can be purchased in most fabric shops. The maternity panel is precut, so if there is a zipper in your pants, make sure you have a panel large enough to cover the required area when you cut the zipper out.

Step 1 Lay your panel on your pants and mark its outline with marking chalk or a fabric pen. (Fig. 274.)

Step 2 Use a ruler to mark a second line ¾ inch inside the outline of the maternity panel. Cut along this line. (Fig. 275.)

Step 3 Turn the raw edges under ½ inch, slashing the corners to make this possible, and pin or baste. Then, topstitch on all sides. (Fig. 276.)

Step 4 Insert the maternity panel, pin, and topstitch in place. (Fig. 277.)

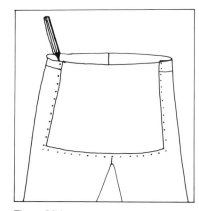

Figure 274

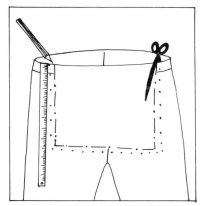

Figure 275

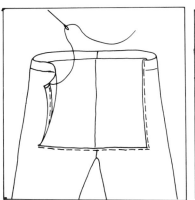

Figure 276

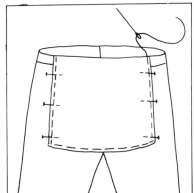

Figure 277

Altering Pants

Materials	Your favorite pair of pants or jeans. Two panels of fabric, 6 inches wide and 1 inch longer than the measurement from the waistband to the turned down hem.

You may find that in addition to adding a maternity panel, you may need to adjust your pants through the hips and in the legs. This is done by adding a panel of fabric along the leg seams. Be sure that you choose a fabric that not only looks good with your pants, but that also has the same cleaning requirements.

Step 1   Let the hems out of both pants legs. (Fig. 279.)

Step 2   Open leg seams on the side, cutting through the waistband if necessary. If you do cut through the waistband, turn under the raw edges and a bit of the edge below the band and merge it gradually with the seamline. Iron flat. (Fig. 280.)

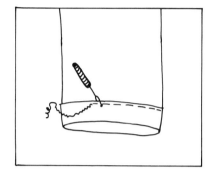

Figure 279

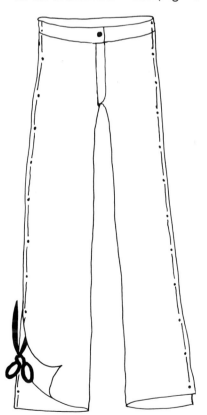

Figure 280

Step 3   Turn one side and the top edge of your fabric panels under ½ inch and press flat. Turn under another ½ inch and press. (Fig. 281.)

Step 4   With the turned under edge at the waistband, pin the folded under edges of your fabric panels to back seam edges. Stitch in place. (Fig. 282.)

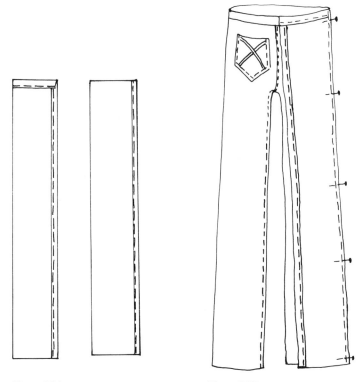

Figure 281   Figure 282

Step 5   Put the pants on by pinning them together so that the pants fit comfortably. Remove the pants and finish pinning the fabric panels to the front edge of the seam so that both sides are even. Try them on once more to check the fit. Make any necessary adjustments.

Step 6   If you have not used the full 6 inches of panel, trim away the excess, leaving a 1-inch margin. Turn the raw edges under ½ inch, and press flat. Turn under another ½ inch, press again, and stitch in place. (Fig. 283.)

Step 7   Hem your pants and they're ready to wear. (Fig. 284.)

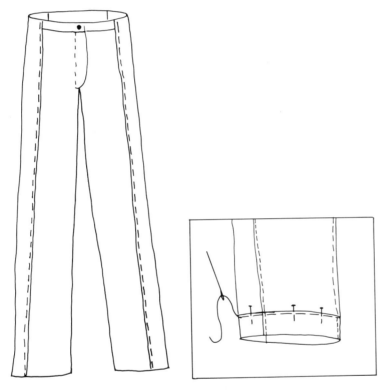

Figure 283   **Figure 284**